Dorothee Soelle—
Mystic and Rebel

Dorothee Soelle—Mystic and Rebel

THE BIOGRAPHY

Renate Wind

Translated and Edited
by Nancy Lukens and Martin Rumscheidt

für Rachel in Freundschaft
Nancy

Fortress Press
Minneapolis

DOROTHEE SOELLE—MYSTIC AND REBEL
The Biography

Cover art: B. Friedrich-Ullstein bild/The Granger Collection
Cover design: Laurie Ingram
Book design: PerfecType, Nashville, TN

Library of Congress Cataloging-in-Publication Data is available

The paper used in this publication meets the minimum requirements of American National Standard for Information Sciences—Permanence of Paper for Printed Library Materials, ANSI Z329.48-1984.
Manufactured in the U.S.A.

16 15 14 13 12 1 2 3 4 5 6 7 8 9 10

Contents

Preface to the English Edition

We are honored to have the opportunity to make accessible to the English-speaking world Renate Wind's biography of our late colleague and beloved friend Dorothee Soelle. In working with this text we have discovered how urgent the questions engaged and lived by Soelle still are, and with what skill and insight her biographer conveys that evolving journey of seeking God through prayer, poetry and action, resisting violence and injustice out of compassion for God's people in a suffering world.

Dorothee Soelle, arguably one of the most important twentieth century German women theologians, is known to many in the United States, Canada, and Latin America who encountered her during her twelve-year professorship (1975–1997) at New York's Union Theological Seminary, her appearances during international lecture tours, or in the context of her decades of peacemaking efforts. Some readers will be familiar with the twenty-five books by Soelle in English translation (see Works Cited on page 193), including *Against the Wind: Memoir of a Radical Christian* (1999) and her major work, *The Silent Cry: Mysticism and Resistance* (2001). Despite numerous academic studies of her work, Renate Wind has written the first biography of Soelle in German or English. It is a task whose time had come, for the generation of her contemporaries is no longer young.

Moreover, we are persuaded that Generations X, Y, and those to follow, as well as any elders who have not had the good fortune to know of Soelle until now, will be well served by Wind's succinct and powerful account and may be encouraged to discover Soelle for themselves. No English equivalent exists of her twelve-volume collected works (Gesammelte Werke) published from 2006 to 2010 by Kreuz Verlag nor of many works we quote in translation. We hope that will change.

One previously unpublished Soelle poem, "Heart Attack" (April 1981), is included here, having been generously provided to the author by Professor Tom Driver of Union Seminary, New York, after the German publication of the biography in 2008. This book also includes many previously unpublished photos and texts discovered by Renate Wind in collaboration with Fulbert Steffensky in the family's archive.

Dorothee Soelle was not only a theologian and teacher, a contemplative and a peace activist—"mystic and rebel"—but also a reader of literature, a lover of hymns, songs, and poems, and herself a poet. Soelle's poetry and the songs and poems she translates or cites are scattered in many different publications, whether within her own work, sometimes untitled, or cited in essays about her, sermons, workshop or worship handouts, church newsletters or websites. No single collection of Soelle's poetry exists in English. We are pleased that Renate Wind addresses the integral role that Soelle's "theopoetics" plays in her intellectual, theological, and spiritual development as she reaches beyond the sphere of insight and spiritual experience she feels can be articulated in linear, rational terms.

Regarding our translation and editing process, we have made every effort to locate existing translations of the poems and parts of poems cited in this volume. All translations of Soelle's published poetry not credited exclusively to another English publication, or not indicated to be altered versions of these, are our own. Scripture quotations are from the NRSV unless otherwise noted. Our brief parenthetical notes and insertions in the text and our translators' footnotes within the chapters provide information to readers who may be less familiar with movements, institutions, or events of the time period in question than the author's German-speaking audience. For source citations, we have indicated existing translations of quoted material whenever possible. Where none exists, none was located, or where existing translations required alteration or replacement for reasons of accuracy or completeness, we have indicated that in the notes.

This book is a collaborative effort. One of us is a native speaker of German and one of English, one a theologian and one a language, literature, and translation professional. We each translated half the chapters, checking each other's first drafts, revising and rereading several revised drafts, conferring frequently about troublesome phrases and contexts, consulting our various resources, and taking joy in finding answers. Martin Rumscheidt searched existing works by Soelle in German and English for cited material; Nancy Lukens searched other cited works, prepared the front and back matter and many footnotes, and edited the text.

Finally, we commend to the reader Renate Wind's characterization of Soelle, whom she criticizes where appropriate yet whose dream—of justice and peace as a force united to preserve the integrity of creation—she is inspired to share with a new generation:

> One cannot speak of Dorothee Soelle without dreaming the dream that the world might yet be able to find its true order after all; that all God's creatures might live together free of violence, without human beings or nature being destroyed; that life and work might return to a human scale and that life in abundance would not be the luxury for the few that it now is, but possible for all, so that the biblical Shalom might become reality, where justice and peace are united forever.[1]

Nancy Lukens and Martin Rumscheidt

Preface

She wanted to know the truth, so she studied theology. At first it was an intellectual adventure, but it became the beginning of a lifelong journey, an adventure consisting of the search for a home and an identity, for God and God's realm of "Shalom." Somewhere along this path it became clear to Dorothee Soelle that truth cannot be defined abstractly, but must be lived and experienced in the flesh. "Make me to know your ways, O God; teach me your paths. Lead me in your truth, and teach me," says Psalm 24. She opened herself to this way, which led her into the world and into a radical praxis in life. From there she gained new perspectives about God and God's truth.

This biography traces the stations of this life's journey. It attempts to describe the particular historical moments during which Dorothee Soelle's life undergoes further development or reverses direction, or when a new theme or a new challenge enters into her life. For events and developments at such focal points in her life are always connected with what is happening concurrently on the stage of history. At these important junctures, what she considers important is never merely her own personal situation, but rather, as the saying goes in German, when friends get together and talk about everything under the sun—what counts are "God and the world." When

Dorothee Soelle began to write books and poetry and to enter the public sphere with actions like the Political Evensong,[1] she became a historical figure who not only reflected theologically, politically, and poetically about the revolutionary changes and movements of her time but one who initiated, inspired, and embodied these changes.

A person who lives this way has kindred spirits all over the world. There is hardly a familiar name among prominent critical voices in the ecumenical world or in the realm of political and cultural work that does not show up in the same context when Dorothee Soelle is mentioned. They cannot all be listed here. Some will be named because they are part of a particular moment in Soelle's development or because they tell a particular story. The two most important witnesses to her life are an exception: Fulbert Steffensky,[2] her "laughing and crying partner," and Luise Schottroff,[3] her best friend.

I am indebted to these two for the abundance of previously unpublished photographs, documents, and stories. I would also like to thank them for entrusting this project to me, for I hardly belong to her "inner circle," was not a friend, student, nor companion, but at most a younger contemporary, engaged since 1965 in the peace and solidarity movement. There I met Dorothee Soelle again and again, whether as a "grassroots" activist at events protesting the war in Vietnam, or in support of Nicaragua, or at actions of the working group for Peace and Disarmament and at gatherings of the Christian Peace Conference.[4] It was not until the 1995 Hamburg *Kirchentag*[5] that I met her in person, when I was invited to her home in Hamburg to join in an intensive and interesting evening with none-but-prominent "names." But once there, the people I met were simply happy and unconventional people. This made me conscious of other aspects of Dorothee Soelle, whom I had until then known only as the quintessence of a charismatic and sometimes very disciplined fighting spirit.

Since then I have continued in the role of one of her younger contemporaries, by giving the address at her seventieth birthday celebration and in the many memorial events after her death. It is from this perspective that this book, too, is written. It makes no claim to completeness; there are many other important theological and spiritual appraisals of her that would fill volumes by themselves. My view of Dorothee Soelle is characterized by our shared dream of a world in which life, love, and work are given their due place, a world that should be a place of "abundant life," of justice and peace for human beings and for nature. What I share with her are the experiences of political movements that intend to translate this dream into social structures—experiences of liberation as well as limitation—in which Christians, too, have found their place. The future will show how much has survived of these efforts and continues underground. The same is true of Dorothee Soelle's texts and poetry. As a poetic rebel and a prophetic mystic, however, she has already earned a special place in the history of the church and in our memory.

In the end, she herself wanted to be nothing more than "a drop in the ocean" of God's love. It is for this that I especially admire and love her.

Illustrations

1

Dream Me, God

It's not you who should solve my problems, God,
but I yours, God of the asylum-seekers.
It's not you who should feed the hungry,
but I who should protect your children
from the terror of the banks and armies.
It's not you who should make room for the refugees,
but I who should receive you,
hardly hidden God of the desolate.

You dreamed me, God,
practicing walking upright
and learning to kneel down
more beautiful than I am now,
happier than I dare to be
freer than our country allows.

Don't stop dreaming me, God.
I don't want to stop remembering
that I am your tree,
planted by the streams
of living water.[1]

Dorothee Soelle, Activist for Peace and Justice[2]

All of a sudden there she stood, one of 180,000 people who had come to Hasselbach in the Hunsrück Mountains to demonstrate against the United States's recent stationing of new cruise and Pershing nuclear missiles. She had probably spoken at one of many rallies leading up to the Hasselbach demonstration, since she was one of the prominent supporters of the peace movement. But now she simply stood in front of the large music stage, dressed and equipped for long walks on foot, unpredictable weather, and every possible emergency like everyone else at such huge demonstrations. It was October 11, 1986, a clear, sunny day, and the colors and smells of autumn matched the mood that had spread at this most peaceful of all major events of those years; they matched this hope "in spite of everything" that united people from all walks of life and generations on this day.

The peace movement had not been able to prevent the stationing of the latest generation of nuclear weapons in Germany. Nevertheless a lot was happening. The logic of the Cold War seemed to have reached a dead end. From the Soviet Union there were signs of change, détente and disarmament, a gesture of rapprochement that the politicians and military strategists in the West would not be able to get around. Among the performers at the huge outdoor lawn concert, beside many other musicians, was a well-known Moscow rock singer who had come to Germany to sing for the German peace movement together with the German youth idol, singer-songwriter Udo Lindenberg. Afterward, a Russian guest spoke; strange and beautiful sounds were heard wafting into the autumn sky. "What a beautiful language," said Dorothee, moved by this conciliatory moment in gesture, speech, and song in the meeting of "Cold War enemies" Lindenberg and the Russian guest.

Sometimes the clearest memory of a person such as Dorothee coincides with a specific moment. For me, that particular moment was the time when the song about the "Wind of Change"[3] took over the hit lists and when the Conciliar Process for Justice, Peace, and Integrity of Creation[4] took over the churches. It was a time when musicians and writers enriched the efforts to create a different world through art and culture and in the process revived the traditions of earlier peace movements. The following short, moving song was used to conclude every concert program by two women artists who, like many other cultural groups, accompanied the actions of the peace and solidarity movement.

I hold you in my arm's embrace.
Like seed corn, Hope has grown apace.
Will the dream come true of those who died
for the good we scarcely dreamed could be—
To live without Fear.[5]

And somewhere a poem from the 1950s by East German icon of the West German Left Johannes R. Becher reappears describing the inferno of world wars and the necessity of struggling for peace. At the end of the poem, Becher writes:

Looking back
Seeing through the Present
the Gaze
Turns
Toward the Future,
Sifting what's human:
Free,
Simple,
Beautiful,
Arisen from the dream
of the centuries.[6]

"Dream me, God," wrote Dorothee Soelle, freer, happier, more beautiful—in the end these are the same dreams that unite the radical Christian with the militant Communist but with one essential difference: in her text the human being does not develop as an ideal figure[7] but is created from God's dream. History had more than abundantly documented the limits of human autonomy and of human capacity for the good. For Dorothee Soelle this knowledge of human limitation signaled the necessity of reconnecting with God, enabling and requiring greater freedom and responsibility in the world. For her, "bowing down before God" and "learning to walk upright" were the two poles of her existence, always to be held in balance between pride and humility, revolutionary activism and mystical devotion to God. She wanted to be planted by God in the earth, which she loved, "like a tree by the streams of water." In the end, as if she had chosen the day, the lectionary verse (*Losung*)[8] for the day she died read: "The just are like trees planted by streams of water" (Psalm 1).

Dorothee felt well-grounded in her faith. Perhaps this is why she could hold her head so high, confident of the dream she shared in that moment with so many different kinds of people. They dreamed that the world might yet be set straight, that all of God's creatures might yet be able to live together without violence, without destroying human life and nature, that life and work might return to a human scale and that life in abundance might again become possible for everyone rather than a luxury for a few; that the biblical "Shalom" might be realized in which justice and peace are one, forever.

One cannot speak of Dorothee Soelle without speaking of this dream, without bringing back to life this vision that gave her wings as she stood in the field that autumn day and demonstrated for peace—free, simple, and beautiful.

2

Compañera Dorothee Soelle *Presente!*

Dorothee Soelle's seventieth birthday in September 1999 was an ecumenical mega-event celebrated in several places in order to accommodate all her friends, as well as a large audience of interested people. Speakers from Latin America, the United States, East and West Germany, Switzerland, and France delivered the celebratory lectures. Latin American Liberation Theology was represented, as were feminist theologians from all over the world; grassroots movements in the United States, Christians for Socialism, activists from the Peace and Solidarity movement, and representatives of a new mystical movement—they were all celebrating a woman who, feisty and fragile, had helped to carry along and inspire all these movements and who embodied a new way to live and conceive Christian faith. Not many years later, in April 2003, women bishops and mystics, feminists and socialists, social workers and pastors, musicians, writers, and scholars—all of whom had accompanied Dorothee in life—came together once again for the numerous memorial events following her death. Each contributed a different picture to her memory. For some it was the theology of liberation; for others it was feminism. For some it was her theo-poetics or her mysticism more than anything else. Bärbel Wartenberg-Potter, her close friend and companion in the struggle, best summed up Dorothee: "She combined all of these things, and above all, from day one she was both a mystic and a rebel."[1]

Dorothee Soelle's theological thought cannot be described in the sense of an abstract system of doctrine. Instead, everything she thought and wrote as a theologian arose from living relationships and life contexts; everything had a sensual and bodily dimension and could not be separated from her existence as a contemporary human being who lived and, at times, suffered. She did not speak of God in static concepts but in terms of action verbs: think God, seek God, love God. By doing theology in this way—sensually, poetically, confrontationally—she moved and provoked people. As an emancipated woman, she attacked a church dominated by men; as a convinced socialist, she attacked the established powers in business and politics. But she also provoked God and allowed herself to be provoked by God. This reciprocal relationship unites her with the mystics of earlier centuries. She was such a living witness of an exciting love for God and for the world that many of her friends remember her as if she were still with them. She is still too alive for them to think of her as a monument from a bygone age. In recalling her, something often happens that she herself enthusiastically and warmly described as having experienced among the Latin American community groups, that people would call out the names of the sisters and brothers who had died or who had been violently killed in the expectation that some of those present would answer for them: "*Presente*! I am here!" Those who are still here must carry on the life and inspiration of those who have gone before.

But in what way can Dorothee Soelle be present? Her husband, Fulbert Steffensky, put it best in his "Afterword to a Life":[2] "This woman is too little dead for me to stop talking with her, asking her questions and having my usual arguments with her. She is dead, and she lives. She is silenced, and many hear her voice."[3] This is the kind of lively give and take that she surely meant and wished for when she wrote in her last book, *Mysticism and Resistance*, "With the word 'mysticism,' I try in a twofold sense to name a process in which I find myself: the discovery of traditions of mysticism and their appropriation. To make something one's own also means to re-collect it in the sense of internalizing it.[4] When I read how mystics thought, dreamed, spoke and lived, my own life looks more and more mystical and amazing to me. It is as if I were growing other ears, a third eye, wings of the dawn. I understand myself better because I learn from these 'brothers and sisters of the free spirit' a language that brings my own experience closer to me and lets them shine more brightly. . . . To read the mystical texts is to recognize oneself anew—a being that is buried under rubble. . . . I'm not interested in admiring the mystics. Instead my wish is to let them re-collect me so that I see the Inner Light as clearly as possible every day. It is hidden within me, too."[5] Pierre Stutz later called Dorothee "the little sister of Mysticism," suggesting that she "democratized" both mysticism and theology, making them comprehensible and accessible for many people.[6] And thus many will recollect their own inner light through her, but that is not all. For Dorothee Soelle the mystical love of God is indissolubly bound up with the longing for a better world. She was a path-breaker and a torch carrier, a symbol and a role model with whom many identified, an enlightened and therefore a politically active, fighting woman. She stood just as much for the "Political Evensong" as for blockading military bases to protest the stationing of nuclear missiles. She placed signs of hope along the way for all who wanted to set out for the promised land of freedom, equality, and brother-and-sisterhood but who often enough found themselves back in the desert. She accompanied the processes of liberation and emancipation of a restless generation in all its contradictoriness as it started on its way. She brought a spiritual dimension to the resistance against the structures of violence that reaches beyond the successes and defeats of the day. She left the church of the patriarchs and the ivory tower of academic theology and offered people new ways of reading the Bible. Whoever heard her at rallies or discussions, at *Kirchentag* gatherings or demonstrations, will remember the decisive tone of her voice and the infectious power of her words. She was a witness for the prosecution and an advocate for liberation. Whoever experienced her in this role will forget neither her arguments against male dominance and the rationale for bombs, nor her calls for solidarity with the Mothers of the Disappeared[7] in Chile and El Salvador's martyred church.

But Dorothee cannot be understood merely as the quintessence of women's power and charismatic militancy, much as she repeatedly created this impression. Perhaps many people would have better understood and appreciated what she had to say if she had more clearly articulated in public what she does not hide in her personal memoirs, namely the tension even in her own life, between credible engagement for justice for assuring a future of life on earth on the one hand,[8] and on the other hand the search for God, God's path and God's truth, which poses itself ever anew. Fulbert—who presumably knew her best at the end—told her often, "The nicest thing about you is your contradictoriness." He went on to say, "People who are full of contradictions are people who thirst for something. They will not put up with being labeled by others and told what their limits are. They thirst for more; they are not satisfied with themselves in their own character but claim the right to be, to become a different person. And so they are never quite at home in themselves. They are not good companions in the countries where they live; they are homeless in their own being."[9] But precisely this sense of uprootedness gives Dorothee Soelle her great theme, the cantus firmus that continues throughout her life: the search and the longing for home and identity.

In journeying through the entire body of Dorothee's works one can accompany her on this search. In so doing one is confronted with the new beginnings, the hopes and dreams, the disappointments, doubts, and defeats, and the spirit of resistance of an entire era. The theologian Dorothee Soelle was always inseparable from the contemporary citizen Dorothee Soelle who took seriously Karl Barth's[10] familiar demand that good Christians get up every morning and open the Bible with one hand and the newspaper with the other. The Bible taught Dorothee to speak about God. The news confronted her with the world as a place that is still filled with and determined by violence, where talking about God must prove itself worthy in the face of the history of violence. From Dietrich Bonhoeffer she adopted the challenge to learn "to see the great events of world history from below, from the perspective . . . of those who suffer."[11] But ultimately, mystical "attentiveness" to all that exists is also the prerequisite for speaking about what is hidden within all that exists, for the spiritual dimension of the everyday and the worldly, of God behind and in all things. And such attentiveness ultimately leads to the insight of Rosa Luxemburg, still relevant today, that the first and most decisive revolutionary act consists of saying what is!

Piety and political action were inseparable for Dorothee Soelle. Love of one's neighbor and solidarity, the personal and the structural forms of love, respectively, were for her the powers that hold the world together at its very core, for which it is worth struggling and suffering as well. She "never thought or uttered a religious sentence that she didn't also think all the way through for its political consequences. But there was a center to her faith that could not be instrumentalized," writes Fulbert Steffensky at the end of his "Afterword to a Life": "There was hardly anything she loved more than the *sunder warumbe* (without a 'why')"[12] of Meister Eckhart.[13] And she quoted this verse in her last lecture, two days before her death:

Die Ros' ist ohn' Warum	The rose, it knows no why
Sie blühet, weil sie blühet	It blooms because it blooms
Sie acht nicht ihrer selbst	It looks not on itself
Fragt nicht, ob man sie siehet.	Asks not if you can see it.

3

In the Darkness of a German Romantic Youth

Hildegard Nipperdey with Dorothee, the fourth of her five children

They called her Matchstick. Dorothee, the skinny little girl who didn't want to grow up. "Being a child was all I had known," she recalled in her memoir; "Why should I leave behind the Land of No Fear—my childhood?"[1]

Her father worried: "The child's not growing! She's not growing!"[2]

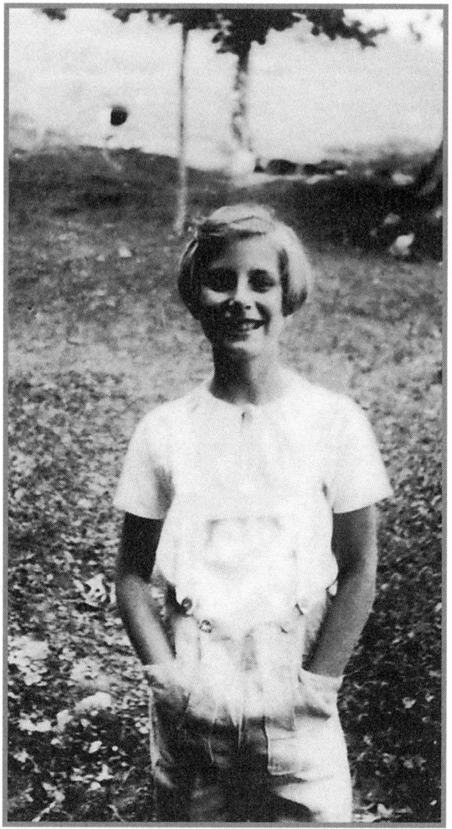

A girl who would rather be a boy

Dorothee was born on September 30, 1929, the fourth of five children of Hans Carl and Hildegard Nipperdey. She had three older brothers and one younger sister. Her father was an attorney, a professor of labor law, and later President of the Labor Court. He was rarely home and was not often present in his children's life. The responsibility for their upbringing and for managing the family's home fell to their mother; she was the center of the family and of their upper-middle-class household. By marrying early and having five children she gave up her dream of a university education and a career. Dorothee would later resolve not to allow this to happen to her. She was deeply connected to her mother throughout her life, but their ideas about life would remain at opposite ends of the spectrum in many respects.

To begin with, the little girl really wished she were a boy. "My mother said that men are better off, except for one thing. They can't have children. I did not find having children as important as going to sea or hacking one's way through the jungle and living in a tree house." At twelve the lanky young girl developed small but conspicuous breasts. "This came as a shock. . . I was born and destined to be a girl."[3] She could not escape her female body, but she was able to escape traditionally female roles. She did not play house with her dolls; instead she took them on adventurous journeys, as she would do later with her own four children.

What goes on at this difficult stage in a girl who doesn't want to be a girl? "Puberty was an intrusion defined by fear. . . . What was very real for me was the fear of not finding the meaning of life . . . of not being a whole person, but merely half."[4] It was like being thrown out of Paradise, being cast adrift in a world that was not the kind of place to live free from fear.

It was 1941, the second year of the war, and the terrors of this war had not made themselves felt to any great degree in the Nipperdey home. Dorothee's family lived in the Marienburg district, one of Cologne's most affluent suburbs, inhabited mostly by professors, with spacious homes surrounded by gardens and parks. The neighborhood was comprised of social equals and like-minded people, liberally educated with conservative upper-middle-class values. Dorothee's father was by no means a friend of the Nazis, but he found a way to accommodate his situation to those in power in the Third Reich. As a labor attorney, he would eventually support the "Führer principle"[5] in the industrial labor organization and ensure its legal footing. This did not hurt Professor Nipperdey's later career in the Federal Republic. When critical lawyers attacked him after the war because of his involvement in the Nazi regime, his daughter Dorothee would defend him. In a letter to the editor of the *Frankfurter Rundschau* published on September 25, 1985, Dorothee wrote: "My father may have participated in the blindness of German legal traditions, both in his commitment to the State and in his relationship to the Labor Movement. . . . My father, who was never in the Party, continued traditions of the practice of law as a German attorney under Hitler and afterward that I consider dangerous; he was not a 'Nazi' in the philosophical and political sense of the word."

Dorothee's memoir points to the contrast that existed for so many families of the German educated elite, between the "exterior" world they experienced in public and the world they could construct in private.[6] At home, or safer places like forest trails with those you trusted, you actually expressed contempt for the Nazis, you rejected their racial ideology, their national megalomania, and their lack of culture. But at the same time, you really did want to take part in shaping things, to benefit from the achievements of the Reich, and you could not and did not dare endanger yourself and your family by openly opposing the regime. The dilemma of the educated middle class, the non-Jewish elite, was the Nipperdeys' dilemma as well: they could not bring themselves to emigrate, nor were they forced to; they could not, nor did they want to join the underground anti-Nazi resistance, nor did they choose the silence of refusal.[7] Yet at the same time, they enjoyed the advantages that such choices allowed them. With such an existence, your living standard was never threatened, you enjoyed a lifestyle appropriate to your class, holidays in the Bavarian countryside near Berchtesgaden that was favored at the time by prominent Germans. Yet, the inner world in which the family and close friends thought and spoke was different from what went on outside. They listened secretly to the foreign radio broadcasts; Nobel laureate and German writer Thomas Mann, a staunch anti-fascist, visited their living room via his talks to "German Listeners" from his exile in California. People warned their Jewish friends and colleagues; there was talk about concentration camps and deportation. The Jewish mother of a Nipperdey family friend was hidden for six weeks in their attic room.

Dorothee's memories of the horrors of the Hitler years remained strangely contradictory. At the time, she wrote hardly anything in her journal about that "exterior world" of Nazi reality that involved being on one's guard, nothing about her father's public role, nothing about her own life as a young girl experiencing that outside world in the final years of the Third Reich. Yes, she recalled the years when the Nipperdeys, too, felt the effects of the war, when the bombs finally destroyed even the residential districts of Cologne that had been untouched until then. She remembered evacuation, hunger, and scavenging for food, remembered the Jewish woman hiding in the attic with her glass flask, remembered the poison that was in the flask, remembered the girl in the streetcar with the yellow star. But at the same time, there was an "interior world" that looked so very different and had hardly anything to do with what was happening outside.

While she seemed completely unaffected by what was happening "outside," what grew and blossomed in Dorothee's "inner" world was the "blue flower"[8] of German Romanticism. In that world, one had nothing but contempt for the primitive ideology of National Socialism. But one still was susceptible to the more sublimated form of the same ideology, the "Germany Myth" that the educated German elite with its conservative cultural values had always held dear. This class consciously rejected everything modern. Modernism existed far from the social struggles, hardships, and challenges of the industrial world of labor. Instead, the educated elite nurtured a romantic ideal that National Socialist propaganda consciously co-opted. The educated upper-middle-class youth of the Third Reich read the lyric poems of R. M. Rilke.[9] They knew parts of his sentimental *Lay of the Love and Death of Cornet Christopher Rilke* by heart. They loved nature and the poems of the Romantic poet Joseph Eichendorff. They did dramatic readings of Otto Gmelin's 1933 cult book *Konradin reitet* (Conrad Is Riding). For Dorothee and her friends, both male and female, this "rider" became symbolic of a certain feeling about life. The letters Dorothee wrote to everyone who knew the code word all ended with an emphatic "We are riding!—Dorothee." On long hiking trips and at evenings for group singing (*Singabende*), even in the bomb shelter, they sang the whole repertory of the German Youth Movement, everything that seduced you into a world of total harmony. There were German and Nordic folk songs, chorales, songs about the Virgin Mary, but no Swing or Jazz, nothing critical, nothing forbidden by the Nazis, nothing foreign. And in this process the young people felt as if their lifestyle expressed their protest against what they saw as the "stuffy" and "materialistic" world of the adults and against the attitude of Dorothee's parents and her older brother Carl, who were increasingly critical of the Nazi "Germany Myth." Basically, Dorothee and her friends were refusing to confront the real world or to allow a realistic perspective on things to enter into their consciousness. And there were still ways to escape doing so: Dorothee, the daughter from a privileged home, devotedly played the piano—Beethoven and Schubert—and derived comfort from the poet Hölderlin: "But where there is danger, that which saves also grows."[10]

In the memoir she published five decades after the war, Dorothee reflected critically about her diary from the war years:

> Discoveries of the mind, of Beethoven's "Pathétique" and Bach's "Saint Matthew Passsion", of Rilke's *Book of Hours*[11] and Goethe's *Sorrows of Young Werther,*[12] while the political reality of everyday life enters only at the margins. I . . . wonder about the meaning of this web of friendship, feelings, literature and music in which my friends and I lived and moved. Was it an escape from reality? Or did it protect us against it? Was it a "consolation of the world," as one of our favorite poems was called?[13] Who would I be without those years of excessive

> romanticism? To what extent did that romanticism insulate me and create a safe place for me to grow up? To what extent did it seduce me to keep on feeling and thinking the same old lies, just in a more sophisticated form?"[14]

It was surely not easy for Dorothee to confront her own past in the form of her "scrawled" diary in Sütterlin, the old German script. For the diary not only reflected the choice she had made to avoid open confrontation with Nazism in favor of a kind of "inner emigration,"[15] but it also revealed traces of youthful vulnerability to the seductions of the times. Her memory was split in two: In the politically correct formulation of the 1995 memoir we read: "We were always waiting for liberation."[16] In the diary she had written fifty years earlier, there was quite a different tone. There she had described the catastrophe of defeat, the homeland that was no longer allowed to be German, her disappointment with the much-admired writer Ernst Wiechert's September 1945 "Address to German Youth," in which he had challenged them to reflect critically. Dorothee, sixteen years old at the time, had written Wiechert a letter:

> Are they who believed [in National Socialism] really guilty? . . . Is it not correct and natural for youth to believe where others are skeptical, to venerate where others condemn, to sacrifice themselves where others see through it all with their clever eyes? . . . I did not believe the clichés, I believed in Germany. And that is the reason why I am so sad. There is nothing in your words about Germany.[17]

Dorothee thus recorded the tragic downfall of Germany in May of 1945 in her diary and imagined herself as a Joan of Arc in the midst of it all: On May 3, in Jena, anticipating it would soon be occupied by the victorious Russian troops, she wrote: "I am reading and studying Hölderlin, Shakespeare, and Sophocles. I shall forge myself a set of armor. Tomorrow I shall need it."[18]

Among the most important influences from Dorothee's school years immediately after the war, as described in her memoir, is Germaine, her adored teacher. Germaine was one of those idealistic Youth Movement women who saw in National Socialism's backward-looking Romantic utopia, combined with elements of Modernism, new role models women could identify with that were different from the conservative images of women they knew. She held by her ideals, even when facing the occupation authorities in the "denazification" process: "Germaine had to present herself to the school board and later again to the British authorities. It would be terrible were she not allowed to teach any more just because she had joined the Party and the Nazi Girls' Organization, the BDM.[19] Everything she worked and fought for all these decades is now up to the whims of an Englishman! How bitter!"[20]

Apparently, there was no strong counterweight to the influence of this teacher on Dorothee, who became her friend after the authorities fired her from her teaching position. School offered Dorothee neither any enlightenment about Nazism, nor did they process what happened during the Nazi years. Instead, opportunism and preferring to "know nothing" were the rule. Germaine had more credibility in Dorothee's eyes—and she is the first person who noticed the traumatized young woman and took her seriously: "With her I could feel like an adult for the first time."[21] The two women met, listened to Beethoven's cello sonatas, drank coffee, talked about Germany and the times, about love and the meaning of life. And then the following sentences appear in Dorothee's diary of November 1, 1945: "I discovered the other day, by accident, that Daddy is one-quarter Jewish and was subjected to political persecution. At first I was horrified and had such feelings of inferiority; after all I am too 'Nazi-infected' and see the non-Aryan as impure and inferior. So often I think—for example when Germaine is so kind to me—what if she knew this! Surely she would be very disappointed. Ach, this is nonsense! She could get beyond it. After all, it's only an eighth!"[22]

The fact that Dorothee's "Jewish grandmother" remained carefully hidden and never mentioned in the family is not surprising and understandable enough. Her mother made an occasional comment that the children simply found strange: "So what difference would it make if you guys had a little Jewish grandma?"[23] There could hardly be a clearer demonstration of the disconnect between the two worlds of a single existence than these very different statements. Dorothee herself committed them so openly to posterity and described her horror at her youthful blindness as a starting point for a process of personal *Wiedergutmachung* (restitution),[24] adding: "As it turned out, it became a lifelong process, born from a deep sense of shame."[25]

But in 1945 the prevailing feeling had not yet been one of shame. The feeling of victimhood was far stronger than any sense of complicity with the perpetrators. This feeling was reinforced by the personal tragedy the family experienced at the end of the war when Dorothee's oldest brother Carl, a prisoner of war in Russia, died on the train that was to bring him home in November 1945. "When we learned this news shortly before *Totensonntag*[26] 1945, I knew there would be no Christmas nor any pious clichés about the 'dear Lord' either."[27] The children saw their mother nearly break down over the loss of her first child. The privileged world of the upper-middle-class family, protected for so long, was irreparably torn. And for Dorothee, who was studying for her high school graduation exams (*Abitur*) through these post-war years, there would be a gradual, depressing awakening out of that mythical idea of "Germany" and its deceptive fog. But only very slowly did "the darkness of a German, romantic, educated upper-middle-class youth"[28] turn to day.

4

Suspended in Nothingness

Dorothee as a defiant existentialist

Life is a dream. 'Tis waking that kills us.[1] These sentences by Virginia Woolf probably best express what young Dorothee felt as she slowly woke up "into a darkness that had no beginning. . . . In the downfall [of Hitler's regime], what collapsed was not only the Third Reich but also the world that could not prevent or put a stop to it, the world of the German bourgeoisie."[2] Initially, the philosophy of Martin Heidegger provided her with some ground to stand on.[3] On a scrap of paper that lay on her desk for years she noted this sentence of his: "Existence is being suspended in nothingness." At this point she saw neither an alternative to this nothingness nor any real discovery on the horizon. She maintained her rather tragic sense of life. On New Year's Eve 1946 she wrote: "So this year comes to a close, and yet I neither know nor hope for comfort or help from what is to come. We have not yet reached the utter depths of the abyss. Buried in my books, the poet Kleist[4] and the history of the Greeks, I look up sometimes and listen: the prisoners of war are not permitted to return; the Saar[5] is no longer German; the demolition of German industry continues. . . . I continue on my way, without hope, with little faith, a little tired. The only thing that remains constant is the demand for bearing; every bit of courage is needed in face of our state of 'thrown-ness' (*Geworfensein*)."[6]

After World War II, people in intellectual circles liked to speak of their state of being as *Geworfensein* ("being thrown")—using Heidegger's terminology. Redesigning oneself out of nothingness became the watchword of existentialism. This was the voice of Jean-Paul Sartre blowing over from France into the intellectual world of Cologne, creating a counter-melody to what Soelle called "Catholic reactionism. . . . , that triumphalist Catholic blockheadedness of the Rhine region that was widespread in the girls' school I attended."[7] She later reflected in her memoir about this discovery: "Lore and I hear the following words in a lecture on Sartre 'Freedom has struck me like a bolt of lightning! I am my freedom!' This freedom doesn't make life any simpler, but it does make everything more intentional and clear."[8]

As a matter of fact, some things did become simpler for the Germans who heard of the French existentialists' newly discovered freedom, but they did not become more intentional or clear. What the existentialist thinkers were working through with the idea of "redesigning" was their own trauma, their "inner emigration"[9] during the time of the German occupation of France. Existentialism provided the German educated elite new ways of thinking and identifying themselves that largely relieved them of taking responsibility for the catastrophe of fascism. It programmed them instead to speak in terms of a "new beginning." Dorothee Soelle later recalled: "If you did not want to return to the bourgeoisie and its ambivalences, the only option for my generation within the tradition of the middle class was to become a nihilist. Nietzsche, Gottfried Benn, Heidegger, Camus and Sartre were our conversation partners."[10] Christian faith appeared to the eighteen-year-old as "an impermissible escape from the darkness that must be lived through."[11] Instead, the heroic emotions associated with "nothingness" and "freedom" were conjured up, a cloak lined with the Adagio from Beethoven's *Pathéthique*. Was there any better protection from the knowledge of error and failure, from having to deal with the perpetrators and face the victims?

Dorothee was arrogant and yet vulnerable, a know-it-all and yet tirelessly inquiring, seeking answers, horrifying to teachers and pastors, who chose to avoid matters with all-too-simple answers. For a long time she felt she had met no one who conveyed to her a form of Christianity that included critical reflection and an authentic Christian existence. Then one day a teacher appeared in whom she could glimpse for the first time a place to stand in the darkness of a romantic existentialism. She confided to her diary: "The new religion teacher is fabulous—unfortunately a Christian!"[12]

Marie Veit, the teacher with a doctorate in theology who was only a few years older than Dorothee, was not only her intellectual conversation partner but a wise educator. She understood and patiently accepted the impetuous and passionate person the bright eighteen-year-old happened to be at that time. Dorothee later remembered Veit with great respect: "She was a marvelous teacher who never prohibited my cheekiness and bold comments but always required that I be clear. Today I think that she respected my anger and was bemused by my arrogance. Challenging our intelligence, she simply trusted people's capacity for comprehension and conscience."[13] Marie Veit, like Dorothee, came from the bourgeois world of Cologne, but she had quite different experiences from her student. Unlike the Nipperdeys, her family could not or did not want to keep their "Jewish grandmother" secret. Marie Veit recalled the situation during her lecture celebrating the fiftieth anniversary of receiving her doctorate:

> I myself am one-eighth Jewish. Our father was driven from his position as Professor of Anatomy because he was one-quarter Jewish and I experienced how colleagues avoided him, crossed to the other side of the street when we approached, and how my classmates no longer walked the same way to school as I did after he was fired, leaving me to walk alone. You do not forget these things when you've experienced them as a young person. But in the church, in the Confessing Church[14] congregation we belonged to, we were fully accepted. My father was a member of the Council of Brethren[15] in Cologne. Though he was a moderate German National Party loyal from the old days, a close bond of friendship, resistance and hope soon formed between him and the "Red Pastor" of Cologne, Pastor Fritze.[16]

Marie Veit experienced "civil disobedience" for the first time in Confessing Church worship services. In this oppositional context, worshipers also experienced the Bible differently than in the churches that were accommodating the Nazi regime. Here, the Bible was a book filled with "perspectives of hope": "It was the breath of the future that blew on me, that was part and parcel of this book more than anything else . . . Bible and Church—Breath of the Future. Much later I learned how Rudolf Bultmann[17] was asked whether he could say very succinctly and simply what 'God' is. 'O yes,' he replied, 'God is my future.' . . . It was clear to me in that moment: It is so."[18] In 1946 Veit received her doctorate, directed by Bultmann, and after a long hearing by the Rheinland regional Lutheran church leadership, she was hired as a high school religion teacher in Cologne. Without her, Dorothee Soelle "would never have ventured into theology."[19] With Marie Veit, Dorothee experienced a Christianity that was open and critical, that swam against the stream. While the new religion teacher did not avoid Heidegger and Sartre, she added the Apostle Paul and Martin Luther, Dietrich Bonhoeffer[20] and Ruldolf Bultmann as new conversation partners. She introduced Dorothee to a different church tradition, to Christians from the Confessing Church. From her own perspective, she mediated the legacy of the resistance, the view of the victims in the land of the perpetrators.

Marie Veit helped Dorothee Soelle to achieve this shift in perspective, to learn to see the history of the recent past from the perspective of the victims. But this did not make life any easier. Waking up into an existentialist, dark state of "thrown-ness" had been simpler than coming to see the unprecedented crimes against humanity that had in the end led to the German catastrophe and those that had preceded it. This second awakening came after a significant delay, but now Dorothee realized all the more passionately the entanglement of guilt in which she found herself: "I was born the same year as Anne Frank, 1929. I was twenty years old when I read her diary. In 1950, when the first German edition was published, she had already been dead for more than five years."[21] Anne Frank, the young Jewish girl from Germany who fled with her family to Holland and tried to survive the Holocaust there in the back upper room of a house in Amsterdam, became Dorothee's contemporary after the fact from the "other side," the girlfriend who did not survive the gruesome terror. The difficulties and the loneliness of puberty connect the two. "Anne had described exactly what I too had experienced: 'Everyone thinks I'm showing off whenever I open my mouth, ridiculous when I'm silent, insolent when I give an answer. . . . All day long I hear nothing but what an exasperating creature I am, and although I laugh it off and pretend not to mind, I really do mind.' Hadn't my experiences been similar?"[22]

Yet at the same time Dorothee was horrified by the dissimilarity of the worlds in which they lived. "The story of Anne Frank is the exemplary story of one of the victims; she tells what 'going into hiding' means and the ways in which people tried to escape persecution."[23] And there was yet more to her horror in relating to Anne Frank: "The machinery of death to which she was delivered is one that my people conceived, planned, built, oiled, and serviced right to the bitter end. One of the passages I had underlined in my tattered copy of her diary is the following: 'Fine specimens of humanity, these Germans! And to think that I was once one of them! Well, Hitler declared us a people without a country long ago. And there are no greater enemies on earth than *these* Germans and the Jews'. . . How often I have wished that Hitler had also made me 'stateless!' "[24]

The drama of Dorothee's awakening hardly can be better described than with this last sentence. She was very connected with her homeland. In her romantic sentimentality she was focused on the natural landscape she knew and on German culture, and proud to be German. All this suddenly fell apart when the images of Auschwitz entered her consciousness, the rows of naked women, some with children in their arms, on the way to the gas chamber; the mountains of eyeglasses, suitcases, and children's shoes in the murderers' storerooms. The country that had once been a homeland became a place of homelessness; her pride became an "ineradicable shame—the shame of belonging to this people, speaking the language of the concentration camp guards, singing the songs that were also sung by the Hitler Youth and the BDM, the League of German Girls. This shame does not lapse; in fact, it must stay alive."[25] She felt that existential nihilism could not overcome this shame, writing that "it's no place to stay and live"[26] once the great abyss of homelessness has opened up.

Soelle's sense of defiant and tragic suspension in nothingness ended when she began to identify with the victims. "I need this shame about my people; I do not want to forget anything, because forgetting nurtures the illusion that it is possible to become a truly human being without the dead. The truth of the matter is that we need their help. I needed my friend Anne Frank very much."[27]

5

In Search of a New Home

The "great abyss of homelessness" in the philosophical, cultural, spiritual, and emotional sense remained an existential issue for Dorothee as she embarked on university studies in the late 1940s. Where was one to find a sense of "home" (*Heimat*)[1] when the very notions of "parental home" and "homeland" had become alien concepts? What options remained for putting down roots when existential nihilism provided no abiding place? Dorothee explains in her memoir: "In 1949 I began to study classical philology, still under the spell of the German humanist culture that had so fascinated me.[2] I set out to search for my soul in the land of the Greeks.[3] I studied theology in order to 'get at the truth' that had been kept from me long enough. Slowly, a radical Christianity began to nest in me."[4] Before seriously embracing theology she encountered Kierkegaard, whose existential Christianity provided a bridge to the new territory of theology: "I tried to make 'the leap,' as Søren Kierkegaard called it, into the passion for the unconditional, into the reign of God. It was then I began to become a Christian."[5]

This endeavor of honestly probing what God's reign might mean for postwar Germany ran counter to both ecclesial and social reality as they appeared to the increasingly critical student Dorothee Soelle. Most people in the Federal Republic of Germany that was just in the process of being constituted[6] had no time for regret or repentance, so there was in reality no "new beginning." People were busy with the reconstruction of the country that lay in ruins and had no desire to look back in the process. The churches began by restoring their bombed-out buildings and steeples. The liberal bourgeoisie that had been unable or unwilling to prevent fascism believed that it could proceed in 1945 where it had left off in 1933. "How could parents and teachers assume that the bourgeois culture that had expired in Auschwitz was salvageable? What amount of rebuilding, re-educating, re-arming, reconstituting of previous conditions of ownership, and all the other 're-s' could ever save it? . . . How could there be hope for a reconnection without radical surgery?"[7] Later on, Soelle would ask this same question of theology as well, concluding that after Auschwitz one cannot speak of God as before.

But for the time being, Dorothee was a questioning, searching young contemporary who, like others, needed to figure out for herself where she stood. She clearly stood apart from those who represented the new Federal Republic, who decisively advanced their agenda of integrating West Germany into the alliance of victorious Western powers. This agenda soon rendered impossible the reunification of Germany as an independent and neutral nation between the eastern and western blocs of "superpowers." Instead, in the early 1950s a program of rearmament was implemented.

Many who had envisioned a new Germany quite differently resisted this resumption of militarism. A first postwar peace movement headed for the streets in pursuit of their causes. It included leftist and liberal civil rights activists, Socialists and Communists—the latter party, legal at the time, was banned soon thereafter. Last but not least, many from the former Confessing Church who had actively resisted Hitler now joined in the new efforts against the arms race.[8] This group gathered in the 1950s around the small pacifist "All-German Peoples' Party" (*Gesamtdeutsche Volkspartei*) founded by Gustav Heinemann,[9] which rejected rearmament of the Federal

Republic and its integration into the Western military alliance. "Never Again Fascism" and "Never Again War" are the messages that united diverse strands of this early peace movement. By the end of the decade, it had transitioned into the "Easter March" movement against atomic weaponry. Martin Niemoeller,[10] like Gustav Heinemann a leading mind of the Confessing Church, became one of the most important voices in this movement. Among those calling for the Easter marches were also survivors of the German resistance to Hitler and surviving family members of those murdered by the Nazi courts. They marched for peace, only to learn from bitter experience that in postwar Germany, too, they remained marginalized in both church and society. They were the guilty conscience of a nation that was setting up house in the society of the affluent. That society wanted to hear nothing about the past or about alternative paths to the future.

For Dorothee and many others of her generation, by contrast, the living and the dead witnesses of the resistance to Hitler were of utmost importance as companions on their journey, patron saints in a homeland that had become alien to them. How could one have gone on living in Germany without Sophie Scholl and Dietrich Bonhoeffer? Inge Scholl's little booklet about her brother and sister and the other members of the student resistance group the "White Rose" first appeared in the early 1950s. Many years later, Dorothee would write in her introduction to the American edition of that book that these people died so that it would be possible for her to go on living at all in her own country.[11] Inge Scholl's name, too, was among those calling for the Easter Marches; people like her became companions to Dorothee on her journey into a resistance way of life. Soon she too would give her support to the "All-German People's Party" and take part in Easter Marches and peace rallies. In a country that felt like an alien land, where you felt out of place, like a stranger,[12] there began to be a small niche made up of those who thought and lived differently, a little piece of home in the midst of a society that was growing by leaps and bounds economically but remained indifferent to the sufferings of its victims. Volker von Törne, the young lyric poet from Berlin and cofounder of "Action for Reconciliation" (*Versöhnungsbund*), lamented his society's mechanisms of repression in this short and disturbing poem, citing one of the most common anti-Semitic slogans of the Nazi era:

> The Jews are our undoing[13]
> We always said that
> No one knew that[14]

Dorothee wanted to know everything: What happened? Why was it possible for it to happen? She considered the resisters, the victims, the concentration camp survivors, the émigrés returning to Europe. And this was where she began her final rejection of the nihilist existentialism that turned incessantly on itself. Now she moved toward an existential Christianity that challenged her to "leave the observer's position," giving up the apathy of wanting to "see no evil, hear no evil, speak no evil." As she put it, "One loses one's soul through apathy!"[15] At the end of her search, her struggle, she saw "the face of a man, tortured to death two thousand years ago, who did not choose nihilism"[16]—Christ, the archetype of passion and devotion.

After studying classical philology in Cologne and Freiburg for two semesters, Dorothee changed the direction of her studies and her life. She went to Göttingen and enrolled in a doctoral program in theology and literature. Four years later she completed her degree with a dissertation in literary studies on the structure of a nineteenth-century romantic work, *Die Nachtwachen des Bonaventura* (The Night Watches of Bonaventura).[17] Her degree work was actually not associated with any particular vocational goal—she thought of it more in terms of her search for truth. After this, Kierkegaard became her most important literary companion: "the extreme arrogance and the inner humility of his style" fascinated her. "Kierkegaard was . . . a preacher in a secularized society, explaining and defending the Christian faith.

This undertaking is no less absurd for a Christianity accommodated to the bourgeoisie than it is for a world geared up for business."[18] How well this approach to Christianity and secular culture applied to the intellectual and spiritual landscape of the success-oriented Federal Republic of Germany! One of the key thoughts Dorothee admired in Kierkegaard is: "Inanity knows no fear; it is too content, too happy, too void of intellect for fear." Another is: "To be in need of God is humanity's greatest perfection."[19] She concluded: "What Kierkegaard taught me was that without experiencing and embracing dread, there is no way of becoming a human being."[20] Those who refuse to acknowledge dread "continue to cling to bombs and profit margins."[21]

Once at the university in Göttingen, Friedrich Gogarten became Soelle's most important teacher. He too was a scholar living between arrogance and humility. The first book Soelle bought herself was Gogarten's *Die Verkündung Jesu Christi* (The Proclamation of Jesus Christ), published in 1948. "It was written in an idiosyncratic language and advocated a basic theological principle that I readily absorbed: We can speak properly about God or Christ 'only in our own language,' 'and not in one that has come down to us; just as in the case of everything else that belongs to our life and has reality in it," she writes later.[22] To Gogarten's mind, Dorothee was the ideal student, embodying the opinion he often expressed that "a 'well-mannered' child is precisely one who has no 'breeding'[23]; only the ill-mannered child has proper 'breeding,' and that is an irreplaceable 'breed,' touched with audacity!"[24] As a farewell gift, Gogarten bestowed one of his pipes upon the student who had demonstrated a 'manner' of her own.

Theology became a spiritual home for Dorothee in these years; the church did not. It was a rather non-traditional, un-churchly, existential Christianity in which she tried to find her way forward. And somewhere in this milieu—between art and literature, religion and politics, where people sought new values, new paths and ways of life—the well-bred young lady Dorothee Nipperdey, and the young artist with the wonderful abstract paintings and very little money, Dieter Soelle, found each other. In Dorothee's circles people would say he came from "the other side of the tracks." In some ways he probably also represented in part an opposite pole to her upper-middle-class background. In any case they were convinced that love, if strong enough, overcomes the boundaries between different worlds. Beyond this, their connection can be summarized in Dorothy's one sentence: "We became Christians together." Coming from different social circles and economic classes, they nevertheless shared the deep crisis of meaning after the breakdown of a world of romantic illusions among German youth. They shared the search for a new meaning in life; they were "lost children" who gave one another warmth and support. Dieter Soelle was Dorothee's first great love. She was one of the young women who guarded their hearts against non-committal love relationships, wanting to wait for the "one and only."[25] It was a romantic ideal of love and marriage, and the bride looked the part, very young and entirely in white, as if her appearance as a lovely, pure virgin were a last tribute to the lost world of great romantic feelings. Once she became a young mother, by contrast, she looked modern and emancipated; she was one of the first women of her generation who had to combine work and family and who wanted her life to include both. At first the Soelles lived in a small apartment of their own; later they moved into the parents' large house. And it was there that their three children grew up. Martin, born in 1956, Michaela in 1957, and Caroline in 1961. It is her children who did the most to provide Dorothee a home again on earth. "Perhaps it was not until I . . . had a child that I really began to become an adult, rooted in life."[26] Not until then did her time of searching, wandering, and waiting, the restlessness of her youth and the romanticism of her adolescence and young adulthood, come to an end.

In her work, too, Dorothee felt at home. Following in the footsteps of her teacher, Marie Veit, she became an instructor of religion at a girls' high school in Cologne. She was amazingly free to design the curriculum and lesson plans in her subject and introduced her students to themes and topics that are otherwise generally avoided in history and German courses. In her classes students heard about the Third Reich, the Holocaust, the resistance to Hitler. She taught the plays of Bertolt Brecht, who at that time was still banned in West Germany. Moreover, she brought traditional theological subject matter to life from different angles, from the perspective of Jewish philosopher of religion Martin Buber, for example.[27] Beginning in 1960, she had the opportunity to write on theological and literary topics for various radio broadcasts and newspapers.

At this point Dorothee had actually realized a goal toward which she had strived for many years, when suddenly a world fell apart

The very young bride Dorothee, in white from head to toe, marries her first husband, Dieter Soelle.

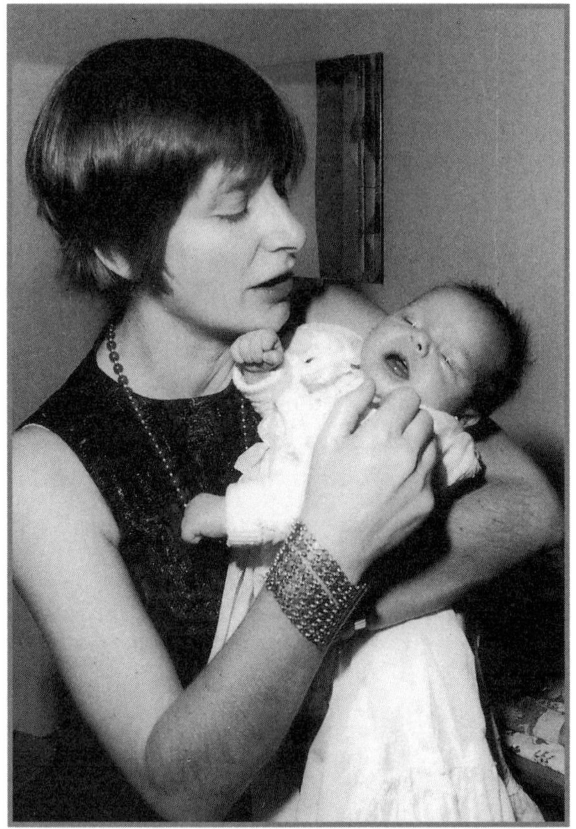

Dorothee Soelle embodies the modern emancipated mother.

for her with her separation from Dieter Soelle. For Dorothee, who thought in absolute terms in matters of love and marriage as well as other things, the break-up of the marriage was a catastrophe. Presumably, it was a relationship that was suited to a particular period of life and then no longer. The notion of partnership for one stage of life, now rather common, was still unheard of in the early 1960s. Divorce at that time meant the end of one's entire life plan. The home she had longingly searched for and apparently found was lost once again.

6

An Essay in Theology after the Death of God

What does the road ahead look like when the questions of home (*Heimat*) and identity must be asked and answered again, but differently this time? What shields people from the angst associated with having one's life come unraveled yet again and never becoming "whole"? But as so often happens, in Dorothee's case, too, the crisis of her separation and divorce turned into the beginning of a new phase of life, an opening onto a new path in life in spite of its many difficulties and challenges. Obstacles included the consistently difficult juggling act that characterizes the existence of a single, working mother of three and that threatened to drive her to physical and emotional exhaustion. Yes, her mother and mother-in-law lightened the burden by helping organize the household and childcare, and, now and then, a live-in au pair girl helped out, but none of these solutions was ideal. Again and again, one of the children reacted to their mother's absence with an attack of high fever. Asked what she wanted to be when she grew up, one daughter replied: "I'm not going to be anything. I'll be a mother!"[1] In spite of such painful moments, Dorothee Soelle held fast to her resolve, described this way in her memoir: "Throughout

Dorothee Soelle in the late 1960s

my conscious life, I have resisted letting people make me feel guilty about combining my work with the tasks of family life. . . . I was very clear about wanting to have children, to share my life with a partner, and to exercise my vocation."[2] Dorothee's mother, who had to make different choices in her younger years, supported her daughter in many ways but also chided her: "You can't have everything in life!" It remained a lifelong conflict between them.

But at the same time, the freedom to live such a life at all was a privilege, endless difficulties notwithstanding. Eventually, Dorothee could afford the time to do some freelance work while also holding a two-year position as teaching assistant at the Philosophical Institute of the Technical University of Aachen. Later, she held an appointment in higher education for several years as an instructor (*Studienrätin*) at the Institute for German Studies of the University of Cologne. Increasingly, she was able to do what she most enjoyed: writing, discussing, and teaching. The only way to live relatively comfortably in this freedom without a husband to look after your financial security, to have spacious living quarters and be free of oppressive worries about where the next month's rent was coming from, was to rely on your own resources. As her daughter Mirjam put it in a retrospective on her mother's life, "After all, it's easier to be independent when there's money." Mirjam remembers a mother who was an immensely devoted family person despite her work and active social engagement. She may have had little time, but what she had was "quality time" for her children when you celebrated "what made the moment special": going for strolls together, reading stories by candlelight.[3] Dorothee's culinary skills, on the other hand, were infamous, not only in her children's memory.

Dorothee discovered later that women in situations similar to hers formed partnerships and communally shared housing, and she regretted only that such solutions were still unthinkable in her day. In those days a divorced or separated woman did not consider herself available for social relationships. "It took me years merely to calmly tell the pediatrician that my husband and I were living apart and that I was responsible for the children, and to ask him, please, to put my name on the invoice, and I'll pay it. It was hard for me to develop that much self-confidence . . . in a society where you feel guilty for the failure of a marriage."[4] She still felt somehow incomplete without a male partner; she became involved for a short time with a married man in order to "come in out of the rain," hoping that her husband would return at some point. When he remarried, their separation was sealed.

In this dramatic phase of her life, Dorothee wrote her first theological book—*Christ the Representative* (*Stellvertretung*)—as a way of finding clarity about herself and managing crises in her life. The time and place in which this book came into being make it abundantly clear that it belongs in a biographical context. The hallmark of Soelle's theological work in general is the fact that it is embedded in the personal and social conduct of the author's own life. It is not intended to document systematic knowledge but rather a thought process and a way of living.

The book's subtitle, which translates as *An Essay in Theology after the Death of God*,[5] was initially rejected by German theological publishers. Only Kreuz Verlag agreed to retain this provocative title, which instantly made the author famous. But Dorothee Soelle was not interested in being provocative; instead, she was focused on the ancient topic of home and identity. She wrote in the introductory section:

> How can one achieve personal identity? That is the question from which this essay starts and which it seeks to relate to the other question: What does Christ mean for our human life? Who am I? How do I find my true self? How am I to live authentically, realize my identity? It is not simply an introverted subjectivity that anxiously asks such questions. They are the questions of people in society, a society that claims and shapes them, damages and distorts them. Nonplussed by the setbacks to reality in this century, by the disturbing decline into self-imposed tutelage;[6] dismayed by novel and proliferating versions of the denial of the very possibility of identity; tormented by the neuroses which civilization exacts and which mark its failure to honor its promises of humanization—people look for a world in which it might be easier to achieve personal identity. But every vision of a more congenial world has to be measured against the greatest of them all, the vision of the kingdom of God.[7]

Neither her theological studies nor the church had delivered what this seeker of a place to call home expected from them. True, her teacher Friedrich Gogarten had helped her find a new language, and Rudolf Bultmann, another of her teachers, had opened new, existential access to the biblical message with his theological project of demythologization.[8] But these approaches still left the dimensions of political and social existence largely untouched. Less still could the church—still mired in efforts to restore both physical and organizational structures from pre–World War I—offer a home to people who were seeking new identity and new certainty. For Soelle, Dietrich Bonhoeffer's forward-looking critique held far greater promise: "[E]very attempt to help [the church] develop prematurely into a powerful organization again will only delay its conversion . . . and purification."[9] The German public and the churches had paid just as little regard to Bonhoeffer's call for such conversion and purification, for the confrontation with the church's own failure before the Nazi dictatorship, as his call for it to be "church for others," to "participate in the worldly tasks of life in the community—not dominating but helping and serving."[10] Dorothee Soelle recalled later:

> What enticed me to the life-long attempt to *think* God was neither the church, which I experienced more as a stepmother, nor the intellectual adventure of post-Enlightenment theology. . . . It is the mystical element that will not let go of me. . . . (W)hat I want to live, understand, and share with others is *love for* God. And that seems to be in little demand in these two institutions. At best, what Protestant theology and preaching articulate in what they call 'gospel' can be summed up as follows: God loves, protects, renews, and saves *us*. One rarely hears that this process can be truly experienced only when such love . . . is mutual. That humans love, protect, and save *God* sounds to most people like megalomania or even madness. But the madness of this love is exactly what mystics live on.[11]

For a growing number of human beings, the church in its traditional form was unable to sweep aside the experience of God's non-existence. Bonhoeffer had made this case quite some time before. And for Soelle, the experience of God's absence was dramatically intensified: How can one talk of a God after Auschwitz who, in the words of the hymn, "o'er all things so wondrously reigneth?"[12] What remained after the Holocaust for Soelle was, in her words, "the experience of the end of all immediate certainty, whether objective and universal or subjective and private."[13] Put theologically, what remained was the experience of the "death of God."[14] The experience of the absent God, Soelle asserts in *Christ the Representative,* can be surmounted only by Christ stepping in to fill this empty place. Christ thus "represents" God before human beings and "represents" human beings before God. This is a mutual relationship.

But in this relationship of mutuality, human beings also experience God in Christ in His powerlessness, needing the help of human beings to become knowable. "Christians stand by God in *God's own* pain—*that* distinguishes Christians from heathens"[15] as Bonhoeffer had written in a poem he enclosed with a letter smuggled by a guard from his Berlin prison cell.[16] With *Christ the Representative,* Dorothee Soelle began a lifelong theological dialogue with Dietrich Bonhoeffer.

In a later commentary on this first *Essay in Theology After the Death of God* she writes:

> The answers searched for here are connected with Jesus of Nazareth, "the human being for others," as Bonhoeffer called him. This is how I accomplish the "christological reduction" that is characteristic for the theology of our century. No longer can God be presupposed in the church as the certitude of the heart, as being represented in society. . . . Instead we begin at the godless zero-point that bourgeois society in its development now represents and discover that someone, who encounters us in many sisters and brothers, lived differently than we: Jesus, the brother whom I can understand and yet

who is so far away from me. With him, I can set out on my way without needing some kind of unmediated God-naiveté. . . . If there is a theological-political continuity, it exists for me in this setting out anew with that powerless and suffering One present among us. It is obvious that a victor-christology has little chance of developing out of such a beginning. Not "He

G L A U B E N S B E K E N N T N I S

Ich glaube an Gott, der die Welt nicht fertig geschaffen hat
wie ein Ding, das immer so bleiben muß;
der nicht nach ewigen Gesetzen regiert, die unabänderlich
gelten; nicht nach natürlichen Ordnungen von Armen und Reichen,
Sachverständigen und Uniformierten, Herrschenden und Ausge-
lieferten.

Ich glaube an Gott, der den Widerspruch des Lebendigen will und
die Veränderung aller Zustände durch unsere Arbeit, durch unsere Politik.

Ich glaube an Jesus Christus, der Recht hatte als er "ein ein-
zelner, der nichts machen kann" genau wie wir an der Veränderung aller Zustände arbeitete und darüber zugrunde ging.

An ihm messend erkenne ich wie unsere Intelligenz verkrüppelt,
unsere Phantasie erstickt, unsere Anstrengung vertan ist, weil
wir nicht leben wie er lebte. Jeden Tag habe ich Angst, daß
er umsonst gestorben ist, weil er in unseren Kirchen ver-
scharrt ist, weil wir seine Revolution verraten haben in Ge-
horsam und Angst vor den Behörden.

Ich glaube an Jesus Christus, der aufersteht in unser Leben,
daß wir frei werden von Vorurteilen und Anmaßung, von Angst
und Haß und seine Revolution weitertreiben auf sein Reich hin.

Ich glaube an den Geist, der mit Jesus in die Welt gekommen
ist, an die Gemeinschaft aller Völker und unserer Verantwortung
für das, was aus unserer Erde wird, ein Tal voll Jammer, Hunger und Gewalt oder die Stadt Gottes.

Ich glaube an den gerechten Frieden, der herstellbar ist, an
die Möglichkeit eines sinnvollen Lebens für alle Menschen, an
die Zukunft dieser Welt Gottes.

Amen.

Typescript of Dorothee Soelle's 1969 poem "Credo" (Glaubensbekenntnis, *literally "Confession of Faith")*

> did it and therefore we shall, too," but "He is being crucified every day." To be with him, to hold his image in one's heart and follow him, means to make his perspective on life one's own, that conflicts in essence and unbridgeably with the society in which we live.[17]

The poem "Credo" (also called *Glaubensbekenntnis* or "Confession of Faith"),[18] composed by Dorothee Soelle in 1969, includes the following affirmations:

> I believe in Jesus Christ
> who was right when he
> "an individual who can't do anything,"
> just like us,
> worked to alter every condition
> and came to grief in so doing.
>
> Looking to him I realize
> how our intelligence is crippled,
> our imagination throttled
> and our efforts are in vain
> because we do not live as he did.
> Every day I am afraid
> that he died for nothing
> because he is buried in our churches
> because we have betrayed his revolution
> in our obedience to and fear of the authorities.
>
> I believe in Jesus Christ
> who rises again into our life
> so that we shall be free
> from prejudice and presumptuousness,
> from fear and hate
> and push his revolution onward
> and toward his reign.[19]

7

Encounters in Jerusalem

On the . . . way to Athens, I suddenly realized that I actually wanted to go to Jerusalem,"[1] wrote Dorothee Soelle in her memoir. Jerusalem was not the end of her long path of conversion, but it became an important stop along the way. Not only had she shifted her field of study from classical philosophy to theology. In addition, at this turning point in her life she was leaving behind the theology of the educated bourgeoisie, which adorned itself with the refinement of dogmatic systems and the erudition of exegetical footnotes, but dismissed as matters of mere personal piety the decisive, existential questions: Who is our God? Where is God to be found? In what direction does God want to move us? How can the world be shaped in accordance with God's will? Dorothee perceived that such questions went beyond those raised by scholarly theology into an existential dimension that a "*doctrine* of God" could not really grasp. But it was just these questions that existential philosophy, which had deeply influenced her, asked with urgency, and neither the classical theological system of doctrines nor evangelical fundamentalism could answer them. At this time, numerous Christian women and men were having this experience as they were confronted by the new philosophical currents and the challenges they raised. They had to look elsewhere for answers. For Dorothee, Martin

Buber, the great Jewish scholar and mediator among the different worlds of those who sought God and the truth, was one reason to make a pilgrimage to Jerusalem. She was not the only one hoping to hear answers from Buber that would point a way forward. At the Maria Laach monastery near Cologne there was a Roman Catholic theologian and Benedictine monk who found himself on a similar search, and in fact had embarked on the same route to Martin Buber. In the end, the pilgrimage to Martin Buber brought Dorothee Soelle and Fulbert Steffensky together.

But first they visited Buber individually, neither knowing about the other. At the turn of the year 1959–1960, Dorothee traveled to Israel for the first time; the trip was arranged by the German Society for Christian-Jewish Collaboration (*Gesellschaft für Christlich-Jüdische Zusammenarbeit*). For her, as for many critical Germans of her generation, one aspect of their conversion to a new way of thinking that had become a major focus of action was their interest in and engagement on behalf of the young and vulnerable state of Israel. All the innovations this country was introducing aroused their interest as well—the Socialist-Zionist experiment of the *kibbutz* cooperatives and the transformation of Jewish identity within a modern society that nevertheless remained connected with the ancient traditions and promises of Israel. Dorothee submerged herself in the world of the *kibbutzim*, sought out and met face to face with Holocaust survivors and took in the countryside "that tells the story of the covenant made between God and his people."[2] For the young religion teacher, Christian faith came together with faith in the God of *Israel* for the first time in a profoundly impressive and, at the same time, in a physical way. It was not the Christian sites that attracted her; on the contrary, she was hopelessly alienated by "Holy Land Tourism." She was drawn instead to the Jordan, the Sea of Kinneret, the Judean desert: "My memories are of rocks, trees, light and the rocky cleft. Faith seeks the traces of one's own past. But when I see the specifically Christian places—the Church of the Holy Sepulcher, the Via dolorosa, the myriads of monasteries, priests and nuns, I know then that this is not the place for me, I won't find anything here."[3]

Instead she looked for and found Martin Buber; she had written him a friendly letter and had received an invitation to visit him. "He offered me a chair in his small study and fell silent. I did not know exactly what to say, ask or learn. Finally, it seemed as if an eternity of silence had passed, I stammered something that began with 'I have observed' and went on to question critically the role of orthodoxy in Israel. Buber looked at me and asked how long I had been in the country. It was only my fourth day and I was so ashamed that I wanted to get up, say that 'I am not worthy of being here' and leave. But I decided to venture a second attempt and tell him that I deal with his work in my religion classes—in connection with—of all things!—Luther's 'justification by faith alone,' that I related to his—Buber's—distinction between 'I-You' and 'I-It.' That interested him very much and we then had a really lively conversation. He asked me a question that I understood and that I took to heart only many years later: 'Yes, theo-*logy*, how do you actually do that? There is really no such thing as a *logos* of God!"[4]

At that time, Dorothee Soelle the theologian was still at the beginning of a longer journey that would lead her away from a christology that separates the Messiah Jesus from his Judaism, toward a new perception of the Jewish roots of faith in Jesus, the Messiah. This journey involves turning away from the long-accepted and unquestioned anti-Judaistic way of reading the biblical writings, and from rendering its diverse contents into dogma.

To speak of God, Jewish theologians insist, is not to construct doctrinal systems, but an ongoing discourse, a joint, suspense-filled search for a truth that can never be fully fathomed. Gradually, Dorothee Soelle assumed this stance as well. In the end her discovery of Judaism went hand in hand with her rediscovery of the Torah. But she understood Torah not as burdensome "law," but as guidance and direction, as empowerment for conversion, for turning back and changing one's life. Only such turning back, she found, enables what she called "the right to become someone different." Toward the end of this journey of discovery, Dorothee put it this way during an evening discussion forum at the Oscar Romero House in Lucerne, Switzerland:

> I would like to have the phrase 'the right to become someone different' understood in the sense of an integration into the Jewish tradition that has become stronger and stronger for me. In the course of my theological development I have actually become more and more Jewish. . . . I think that the best we can do as Christians is to become as Jewish as possible. The word that comes to mind in this 'right to become someone different' is a word from the Jewish tradition that I have come to love more and more, the word *teshuvah*, to turn back. The Rabbis teach concerning *teshuvah* that all kinds of things can be *said* about it, but that there is no day and no hour when it is not possible to *do* it. We must suppose, believe, think, and hope that we all, every day and every hour are able to turn back and become different. This is for me the real legacy of Judaism that we Christians, for our part, can draw close to: Christ as our permission to grow into this tradition and as our right to turn back.[5]

The visit with Martin Buber was a first step for Dorothee Soelle on her faith journey. A second step was to follow a few years later. In 1966, she was invited to take part in a conference of the Society for Christian-Jewish Collaboration to be held in Jerusalem. Fulbert Steffensky was one of the organizers; he had visited Martin Buber to discuss with him whether he should "remain in the monastery or leave it." The intellectual challenges to Christianity posed by the new philosophical currents as well as the debate with the newly emerging social sciences were also having an impact at the grass roots of the Roman Catholic church, which was gaining momentum. Protestants

Jerusalem, 21.1.1965.

Sehr werte Doktor Sölle,

Vielen Dank für die Ubersendung Ihres Rundfunkvortrags. Dass ich Ihren beiden Grundthesen - "Gespräch mit Gott" und "Aufs Spiel setzen" - mit ganzem Herzen zustimme, wissen Sie ja wohl. Zu der letzteren möchte ich Sie auf zwei chassidische Geschichten aufmerksam machen, die Sie in meinem Buch "Die Erzählungen der Chassidim" finden : "Der leichte Tod" (S.227) und "Das Wagnis des Gebets" (S.425).

Ich glaube Sie darauf aufmerksam machen zu sollen, dass Sie zu Unrecht - den alten Ubersetzungen folgend - das Wort re'a in 2 Mose, 33,11, durch "Freund" wiedergeben. Das Wort bedeutet hier, wie im Allgemeinen, den Menschen, der uns auf den Wegen unseres Lebens begegnet. Es ist dasselbe Nomen, das im 19. Kap. des 3 Buches Mose durch "der Nächste" wiedergegeben zu werden pflegt - ein leider sehr abgeschliffenes Wort, bei dem man an die wirkliche Nähe gar nicht mehr denkt.

Mit besonderem Interesse habe ich Ihren Aufsatz in "Merkur" gelesen. Er verdiente, zu einem Buch ausgebaut zu werden.

Mit guten Wünschen für Leben und Werk,

Ihr Martin Buber

Letter of the great Jewish philosopher Martin Buber (1878–1965) to the still unknown German theologian

as well as Catholics living at the margins of their churches, finding each other in agreement as an ecumenical group, were searching for new ways of knowing and new sources of knowledge. In the process they discovered their common roots in the Jewish traditions of faith and knowledge of God. It was a manageable process; those involved in this scene knew each other by name. Dorothee Soelle, known by that time through her freelance work in German radio broadcasting and her theological publications, was invited to that conference by Fulbert Steffensky. They arranged to meet at the Zurich airport, enjoyed a getting-acquainted toast of pear schnapps and continued on their flight to Israel. The conference was housed in a Christian hostel in Jerusalem; on the first evening Dorothee, looking for something to drink, landed among a group of critical Catholics in high spirits who had had the foresight to lay in a store of beverages and decided to join this traveling and working group who readily accepted her. The conversation turned to Martin Buber, who had just recently died. Describing the first spark of her relationship with Fulbert Steffensky, Dorothee later wrote: "When we discovered what bound us to Martin Buber, Fulbert suggested spontaneously that we visit Buber's grave together the next day. Everything else had its beginning there in Jerusalem."[6] From Steffensky's perspective, a kind of "veiled affection" blossomed; "from then on the two of us did a number of things together, without any ulterior motives as yet, but every time we got back to the group we were greeted with understanding smiles."[7] Three years later, Dorothee and Fulbert were married. Thus Martin Buber played the *Shadchen* (Yiddish for "matchmaker"), replying after the fact to Fulbert's question about whether to stay in the monastery or to leave.

The marriage caused a minor sensation even though it came as no surprise to the couple's friends and confidants. Having begun in Jerusalem, their relationship soon continued in the form of collaborative action known as the "Political Evensong." This project marked the beginning of a partnership in life and work that was held together by a shared theological and political vision. Dorothee had no use for the then current term *Zweierbeziehung* ("twosome") for an intimate couple's relationship. She often referred to Helene Weigel's and Bertolt Brecht's insistence that what gave meaning and purpose

Dressed in black, Dorothee Soelle marries former Benedictine monk Fulbert Steffensky; it is her second marriage.

to their shared journey was a "third cause" (*dritte Sache*), namely their work and the struggle for justice: "A marriage without common work, without common joy, without a shared vision, suffocates in its own restrictedness." And once again Martin Buber was the marriage broker and counselor:

> Buber's philosophy became very important in my understanding of marriage. In his *I and Thou*, he speaks of two

> basic relationships that constitute human life. One is the relationship of an 'I' to a 'Thou,' the pure and unmediated, language-transcending nearness of one to another. The other relationship is that of the 'I' to an 'It,' the mediated, world-oriented, creative relation to things. Love can renounce world and 'It,' for love knows islands of pure I-Thou encounters. But it seemed to us that marriage happens exactly where the relationship of I-Thou and I-It intersect. . . . We perceived the chances for marriage to be where there is a common field to be cultivated, even one that has not yet come into view.[8]

But Dorothee and Fulbert also share the love of nature, literature, music, and the *joie de vivre.* And it is not only for theological discussion and political action that they come together after their first meeting. "I spent Sunday on a ship on a lake with my mother and her friend, a monk!" little daughter Michaela writes in an essay; that caused a good deal of fuss in Catholic Cologne.[9] A photo of their wedding in 1969 shows the female Protestant theologian in a black mini-dress with her laicized, and by then converted, Protestant former Benedictine husband. There were worlds of difference between the 1954 bride adorned in white and the 1969 bride in black with the "windswept" hairdo that had just become the *dernier cri* in Jean-Luc Godard's first *nouvelle vague* movie. The two contrasting photos are like documents of time-travel through the history of the Federal Republic of Germany. The critical Protestant woman theologian and the leftist Catholic dropout in many ways represented the radical changes in both church and society that occurred in the 1960s. For the first time, priests openly renounced their ordination and, at times, also their church, which firmly clung to celibacy and hierarchical structures.

The media no longer swept the turmoil associated with all these shifts under the rug. The women's magazine *Constanze,* widely read at the time, published an extensive feature article about Fulbert and

Dorothee as well as other ex-priests and their wives. For the immediate families, the event was not exactly one of unalloyed joy. In the case of the "well-bred daughter" Dorothee, people were of course already accustomed to her "oppositional activity," but her second marriage represented yet another twist for those in liberal, anti-clerical circles.

For Fulbert's family, at home in a rural Catholic milieu, it was difficult to comprehend and cope with his leaving an ecclesiastical career and a Catholic vocation. What the popular magazine *Constanze* depicted as a signal of their breaking out into freedom, the Catholic *Bildpost* portrayed as an invasion of sin into the Christian world. This official mass publication, available free of charge in all Catholic parishes, published a scornful and infamous article about this "scandalous couple." Even Fulbert's family found the church paper had gone too far; the extended clan of relatives divided up the job of driving to every Catholic Church in the region and removing every copy of the *Bildpost* on display. It was no longer acceptable to put up with everything emanating from the ecclesiastical authorities, even in the rural Catholic countryside!

In Dorothee's second marriage as well, worlds came together that could hardly have been more different. Fulbert put it like this: "At the time Dorothee became familiar with [Bach's] *Saint Matthew Passion*, I was herding sheep." Dorothee looks back on their marriage with these words: "We playfully draw on the contrasts between us, not only in class and denomination, but also in the customs of everyday life, the songs we sing at Christmas, and the way we try to raise children. For a quarter of a century, Fulbert has had to put up with my far too strong tea, and I with his far too strong coffee; he mocks my 'Protestant fixation with truth,' and I his easygoing 'Catholic imprecision.'"[10] But at the time, the experiment of the "patchwork" family was something new and still unaccustomed. Fulbert became a good father to the three children Dorothee brought to the marriage, and to Mirjam, the daughter they had together. The divorceed couple Dieter Soelle and Dorothee Soelle each found a "home" again and, together with their respective new partners, established a good family community, celebrating Christmas and birthdays together and, in mutual assistance, accompanying the children through the stages of their lives. For Dorothee, Fulbert—whom she called "Steff"—remained her "laughing and crying partner;" he stood by her in the many debates and struggles she was yet to face, making sure that she had space to write and travel. In return he appears in her poems—with laughter and weeping:

For Fulbert

Imbiber and diluter
first and last reader
father confessor in resistance

one who knows the night
and lights candles
to read the book

he protects me
from others and myself
and gives up on no one

except himself at times

compañero[11]

8
Political Evensong

In the beginning, the "Political Evensong" was essentially no more than a discussion group of Protestant and Roman Catholic Christians, both theologians and laypeople, in primarily Roman Catholic Cologne who dealt with religion and culture and wanted to exchange ideas about current political and social issues. It was a kind of Christian variation of the culture and discussion forums that were popular at the time such as the "Club Voltaire." Such groups sought to foster free, more critical thinking in the generally conservative Federal Republic. Those gathering for what became the "Political Evensong" knew one another from the Society for Christian-Jewish Collaboration or from the Easter Marches; they soon realized that dealing with theological issues necessarily leads into political engagement: "Every theological statement must also be a political statement!" It was chiefly the Catholic partners in these conversations who introduced a further dimension to their activities. Inspired by the initiatives of the Second Vatican Council (1962–1965) and the Worker Priest Movement, which was active especially in France, they practiced an approach to prayer and action that the prior of the ecumenical cloister at Taizé, Frère Roger Schutz, called *lutte et contemplation*—struggle and contemplation. This was something to which Protestants were quite unaccustomed; they were

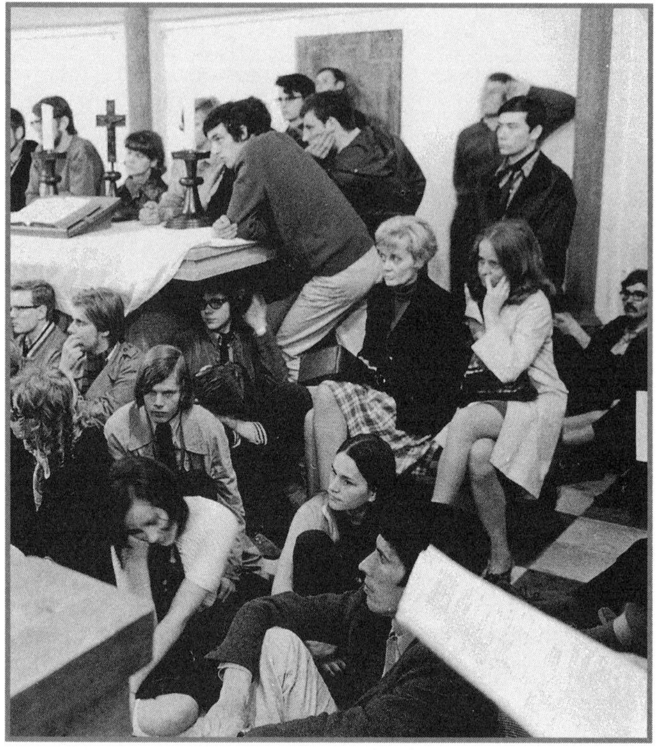

About one thousand people attended every "Political Evensong" meeting in the 1960s and 1970s in a casual atmosphere in Cologne's St. Anthony's Church.

more familiar with discussion of Scripture and of "right doctrine." Yet they were fascinated by this approach. The group experimented with a new form of expression following the principle: "see, judge, act." Their process in the "Political Evensong" was then comprised of four elements: information, meditation, discussion, and action.

The ecumenical Evensong group applied for permission to celebrate a political prayer liturgy about current political issues during the Convocation of Catholics (*Katholikentag*) in 1968 in the city of Essen. The *Katholikentag* administration did not want to turn down the application—after all, a Benedictine priest was to participate—but they scheduled the liturgy for 11:00 pm. And thus the "Politisches Nachtgebet" (literally "political night prayer") got its name. Dorothee described what they did: "Our pattern was to provide political information, to confront the information with biblical texts; someone would give a brief talk, then there would be calls for action, and discussion with the gathered congregation. The basic elements of all subsequent Evensongs were information, meditation, and action."[1] The topics addressed in the late sixties and early seventies were diverse and reflected the upheavals of that time: the war in Vietnam,[2] the crushing of the "Prague Spring,"[3] the intervention of the United States in Santo Domingo,[4] and finally, the fascist putsch in Chile.[5] Societal problems such as discrimination against women, treatment of prisoners, and development aid were also addressed. Each individual topic was prepared by a group in cooperation with experts whom they then involved in the chosen course of action. In this way the initial circle grew ever wider, and friendships developed that transcended the participants' denominational and philosophical boundaries. Maria Mies, later a professor of sociology and women's studies, worked with Dorothee Soelle to plan the Ninth Political Evensong in 1971. The poster motto with its double-entendre announces the feminist focus of the Ninth Evensong with feisty humor: "The Emancipation of Women—Woman Is Still on the Bottom." At the memorial service for Dorothee on June 3, 2003, in the Church of St. Anthony, the same church where the first Evensongs had been held, Maria Mies recalled: "I became politicized by Dorothee Soelle and the Political Evensong . . . Dorothee never did theology for the sake of theology. Her concern was human beings, the creation, and praxis. She would often quote Bertolt Brecht's dictum: 'The truth is concrete.'"[6] Maria Mies also rejected attempts to bring Dorothee Soelle stealthily back into the church, and to gloss over her resistance to being forced into a mold—"to beatify her, so to speak." She reminded people that by that time, their jointly organized Evensongs had long been denied permission to meet in St. Anthony's Church. In fact, both Protestant and Roman Catholic authorities had "locked out" the Evensong from all the churches of Cologne. Perhaps they had forgotten that the churches had never been so full as for these evening gatherings!

On October 2, 1968 the *Kölner Stadtanzeiger*, a Cologne daily paper, reported:

> As early as 8 PM last night, the church of St. Anthony's on the Schildergasse was filled to overflowing. And at 8:30, the parish pastor Jörg Eichert announced through the microphone: "There are still a lot of people outside trying to get in. Let's move closer together, that's a good symbol for an ecumenical worship service." Ten minutes later there was not even any standing room. More than one thousand people had shown up for the Political Evensong in the Protestant church whose pews hardly seat three hundred. There were Catholic priests and curates, Protestant pastors, high school and university students and political activists, for example the Vietnam Circle from St. Alban's Church or the Friends of Biafra Group. People didn't stand on ceremony; they showed up in pants suits and patent leather jackets, put on sunglasses to shield their eyes from the glare of the TV lights, squatted on the floor around the altar or leaned against the pulpit.[7]

Fulbert Steffensky, the Benedictine monk from Maria Laach Monastery, was one of the leading figures and initiators of this first Evensong event, together with Dorothee Soelle. Only a few people knew then that Fulbert and Dorothee had in the meantime fallen in love and become committed to one another.

The photos taken of these early Evensongs by one of Fulbert's fellow monks at Maria Laach convey splendidly the atmosphere of those days. The consecrated space of the church had finally become what it was meant to be, a place of community and reflection. The institutional church was no longer sacrosanct; it was being challenged

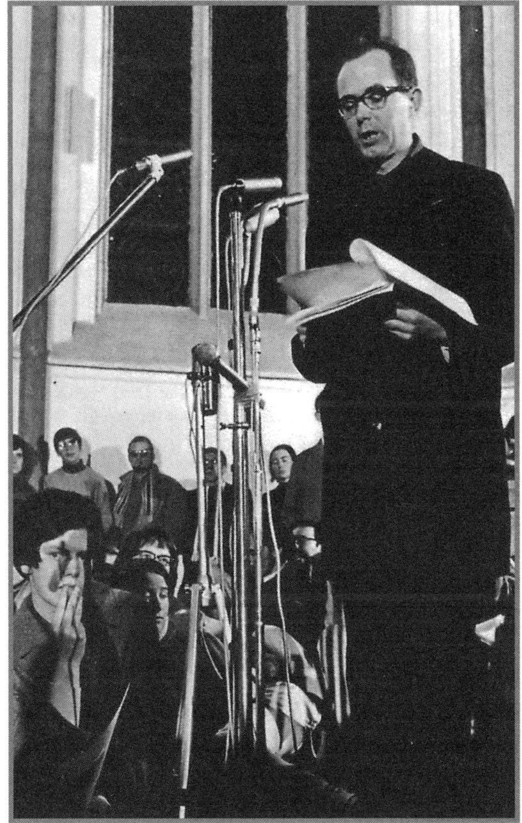

Fulbert Steffensky, together with Dorothee Soelle, was one of the leading Political Evensong thinkers.

with questions about what it was doing for human beings and for their world. For the church authorities, a movement "from below" such as this signified "code red," whereas many other people sensed that the church was finally opening itself again to the world and to human beings, their problems, longings, and hopes. Heinrich Böll, the critical Cologne author and Catholic Christian, wrote an open letter after the Archbishop of Cologne, Cardinal Frings, had denied the Evensong access to the churches:

> Dear Friends, it is beyond comprehension that you have been prohibited to this day from praying your texts in a Catholic church. . . . What you are doing and planning cannot be integrated at all into any of the churches—at least not into any of the currently incorporated churches. You can only be guests, foreign guests, because you do not pursue what every incorporated denomination must pursue: their own "interests." Your engagement in humanizing what the Christian scriptures articulate, and in pushing for society to become a society that embodies humanity, is necessarily "outlandish." Furthermore, the classic representatives of these 'interests' may suspect they smell whatever falsehoods they want in the "Political Evensong," but whatever scent they think they detect, they are mistaken because they have no organs at all with which to sense what is happening here.[8]

Like Cardinal Frings, Joachim Beckmann, President of the (Protestant) regional Church of the Rhineland, also detected a scent of falsehood. For him, as for some other Christians from the tradition of the conservative wing of the Confessing Church, the Political Evensong's linking of the gospel with political causes was comparable to the way the Nazi-friendly German Christians had subverted the church in the years of the "Third Reich." The working group "Political Evensong" responded as follows to that characterization: "The comparison with the Nazi-friendly German Christians is an insult for all participants in the Evensong. Contrary to the rapturous political sentimentality of the German Christians, we strive precisely for clear analysis of factual political situations in order to enlighten and change political consciousness. We represent no specific social philosophy; we do believe, however, that the task of social criticism has thus far not been sufficiently recognized by the churches and by

Christians. In practicing such a critique of our society we pursue an aspect of the Bible and of faith that has been neglected until now, and we meditate and pray about it."[9]

In the meantime, numerous offshoots of the Political Evensong in Cologne were doing exactly this. University student congregations (*Studentengemeinden*) and Christian peace groups in particular embraced the idea that the churches must exercise their critical function in the manner of the biblical prophets by taking on a "prophetic ministry of vigilance" in their diverse life contexts. Citizens formed political groups, critical journals, and action-oriented circles, following the biblical prophet Amos' admonishment that worship becomes blasphemous unless "justice rolls down like waters and righteousness like an ever-flowing stream" (Amos 5:24). Though these groups comprised an active part of the 1968 movements they sought to renew not only society, but the church as well.

To the 1968 generation, Dorothee Soelle provided a new theological perspective and a new language. People who had turned their backs on the traditional church, its appearance and language, now discovered themselves and their world in her texts. With her interest in the arts and literature and her own literary talent as a starting point, she could fashion a language that re-imagined and re-shaped the project of speaking about God in a secularized society. In her 1970 *Thesen über die Kriterien des theologischen Interesses an Literatur* (Thoughts on the Criteria for Theological Interest in Literature), she wrote:

- In the language of art, theology finds a non-religious interpretation of theological concepts.
- Theological concepts are those that represent human beings in their totality and relate them to their eternal life, that is, their authentic life, for example, sin, grace, dying, rising again, justice, peace.
- Theology is called upon to achieve the discovery of non-religious interpretation; mere reduction to theological

nomenclature falls short of meeting that call. Similarly, finding vague parallels between poetic and theological representations fails to provide such interpretation. What longs to be discovered is the substance of the concepts now petrified in religious nomenclature; what longs to be found is how to give them concrete form in the present. "Sin" and "grace" are empty theological formulae whose sole value lies in helping us raise questions, but only non-religious, worldly concretion provides answers to these questions. Only the predicates reveal what the subject is.

- For something to be theologically relevant, it must "[awaken] in us a new way of perceiving" (Goethe), lift us out of the assurance of what we know, confront us with our own clichés, unmask us, change our relation to the world and, hence, our very selves.[10]

Dietrich Bonhoeffer had already recognized that a new language had to be found for the old gospel. In his "Thoughts on the Day of Baptism," he wrote: "In [the] words and action handed down to us, we sense something totally new and revolutionary, but we cannot yet grasp it and express it. This is our own fault. Our church has been fighting during these years only for its self-preservation, as if that were an end in itself. It has become incapable of bringing the word of reconciliation and redemption to humankind and to the world. So the words used before must lose their power, be silenced, and we can be Christians today in only two ways, through prayer and doing justice among human beings."[11]

With these words of Bonhoeffer in mind and while reading Latin American liberation theologian Gustavo Gutierrez,[12] Dorothee Soelle asserted that a new form of proclamation of faith can arise only from a new personal and political praxis. We cannot reflect on what we are not doing! Liberation theology, which was emerging at that same time, was developing this same idea: Orthopraxis has priority over orthodoxy, in the knowledge that again and again, praxis itself becomes the location of insight and understanding. What Gustavo Gutierrez called the first and second act of interpreting the gospel thus became the essence of contemporary theological existence: Only as we live intentionally with and for others, standing up for and in solidarity with others, will Scripture and the gospel open themselves anew to our understanding; only then will new forms and new, authentic words emerge. Dorothee Soelle put this insight into action in her world with courage and consistency: A liberation theology in the context of the "First World."

What did a first-world practice informed by liberation theology look like in those years? Dorothee was indefatigable; she supported and counseled local grassroots groups, gave talks in pubs, back rooms and parish halls of progressive pastors. By now she had become famous and controversial. As a result she was invited to discussions, conferences and organized actions. The diversity of topics she was asked to address created contact with diverse segments of the populations and, for the first time in her life, she came to know and appreciate communists, elderly workers and their wives, all marked by the struggle to resist fascist tendencies in contemporary society and culture. Like everyone who was in the public eye at that time on the social and political Left, she, too, was subjected to the fascist dregs of prejudice and hatred. Anonymous phone calls delivered threats and abuse; terms like "communist pig" were part and parcel of her daily life.

In their public discrediting of Dorothee, both Church and university used all ammunition available to them. This rejection also weighed heavily on her. For Cardinal Frings, her "Credo"[13] was blasphemy; President Beckmann of the Protestant regional churches called it heresy. From the ranks of "orthodox-conservative" (*bekenntnistreu*, literally, "adhering faithfully to a creed") Christians arose the slogan *niedergefahren zur Soelle!*—"descended to Soelle!"—a play on the phrase in the church's classic creed: "descended into hell."

EMANZIPATION
DER FRAUEN

unten . . . Die Frau liegt immer noch unten . . . Die Frau liegt immer noch unte

9. Politisches Nachtgebet

Rheinhausen-Bergheim
Gemeindehaus „Auf dem Wege"
Peschmannstraße

Freitag 12. März 1971 20 Uhr

liegt immer noch unten . . . Die Frau liegt immer noch unten . . . Die Frau lie

Verantwortlich: Arbeitskreis Polit. Nachtgebet Köln/Rheinhausen

The emancipation of women was one of the major topics raised in the Political Evensong. "Woman is still on the bottom!"

Dorothee was able to complete her habilitation dissertation in the Faculty of Philosophy at the University of Cologne, qualifying her for university teaching, despite obstruction from the *Bund Freiheit der Wissenschaft* (Association for Academic Freedom) that had been formed in the universities in opposition to everything on the Left. She had to forget about being nominated or invited to apply for teaching positions; even appointments to non-paid positions triggered a regular culture war such as the one at the University of Mainz. In 1972, on the initiative of New Testament Professor Luise Schottroff and other professors and members of the academic middle ranks, Dorothee Soelle was assigned a teaching position for "theology and literature." Her position caused controversy from the outset and was a non-tenured appointment. When renewal time approached, the conservative fraction, by then well organized, blocked her re-appointment despite the fact that her classes were well attended and the student body supported retaining her. In written recommendations, Helmut Gollwitzer and Ernst Käsemann, both highly respected university professors and theological scholars, refuted the charge that she was "unscholarly." In the end, Luise Schottroff issued a statement that was broadcast on the German television network *Südwestfunk* (SWF):

> Frau Soelle reminds us of the task assigned to us by the Gospel that Christians are to be advocates of *those* human beings who cannot speak themselves or assert themselves: because they are handcuffed by the pressures of work, because they are afraid of losing their job, because the coercion to achieve and produce robs them of their humanity, of their imagination. Frau Soelle shows us that Christians must take sides with the lowly, with ordinary people. The real reasons for Frau Soelle's termination are being suppressed. They are political: Frau Soelle is too leftist. They are theological: Frau Soelle is critical of the perception of God in which God lords it over human beings, beats and chastises them. She says that is a god the powerful wish for. I find her rejection scandalous. What must be said here loudly and clearly is that the freedom of research and teaching is being obstructed—but not by the students. It is conservative professors who are doing this.[14]

Dorothee Soelle the theologian faced a closed door as far as a career in university teaching and research in Germany was concerned. People there had too little imagination to know what to do with this woman who thought against the grain and engaged in activism at the community level. Even Ernst Käsemann, Professor of New Testament and a bedrock of enlightened and critical theology, who actually was sympathetic to her views, once snarled: *Muss sie denn unbedingt immer über die Dörfer gehen?*[15]—Does she really have to make a public statement on every injustice, mobilizing people to action everywhere she goes?[16]

I've heard

I've heard
that saint thomas
recommended three ways
to combat melancholia
sleeping
bathing
and study of the sufferings of christ

I've noticed
that my friends advise
in such cases
sleeping with someone
drinking
and study of one's own suffering

I imagine
other friends
if I could ask them
would recommend
watchfulness
work
and study of a world map
pinpointing illiteracy
and manufacturers of arms

But these friends
whose advice would help
set me right
live far away
behind walls.[17]

9

On n'arrête pas le soleil

YOU CAN'T STOP THE SUN

Dear Friends, Warm greetings from the current 'Capital of Human Dignity.' We spoke to Pham van Dong. He said: 'The sun cannot be stopped!' It's true—and it's also 'myth.' Read Ho Chi Minh's poems and do something for the maimed and mutilated children here. Adieu, Dorothee."[1] Luise and Willy Schottroff received these lines from Hanoi, the capital of North Vietnam, in the fall of 1972.

The first spectacular action of the Political Evensong was a demonstration in 1968 against the war being waged in Vietnam by the United States of America. A group of Protestant and Roman Catholic Christians carried a banner proclaiming: "Vietnam is Golgatha!" through downtown Cologne and propped it up at the entrance to the Cologne Cathedral. The war in Vietnam led numerous people from the peace movement at that time to raise critical questions about the whole Western system. The dark sides of capitalism and imperialism were becoming too evident; people questioned the destructive power of the global market and the violence of a superpower that used its entire military machinery to support a corrupt system in South Vietnam in order to protect its political and

Postcard Greetings from North Vietnam, 1972

economic interests in Southeast Asia. Soon Dorothee Soelle began working with a group called "Action to Assist Vietnam" to organize political and humanitarian assistance for the Vietnamese liberation movement and for North Vietnam, which had also been attacked by the United States. In 1972 she took part in a tour that visited a number of cities and villages in North Vietnam in order to get an impression of the situation in that country. Shortly before the trip, peace discussions had begun in Paris, awakening new hopes for an end to the war. But then–U.S. President Richard Nixon accelerated the course of the war and ordered the bombing of North Vietnam, threatening to bomb Vietnam back into the Stone Age. The results were horrific, especially for the civilian population, on whom United States fighter jets dropped tons of the herbicide with the code-name "Agent Orange." At the time the effects of this toxic chemical were not known, but forty years after the war ended, children in Vietnam are still being born with deformities.

Dorothee was deeply shaken by what she saw. She summarized her impressions in a cycle of poems, *Reiseerfahrungen* (Travel Experiences), most of which appeared in her *Revolutionary Patience* (1974) as "Travel Notes":[2]

> Peace must hide
> it's standing in the bomb shelter a doctor
> searching for shrapnel in the toddler's lung
> it's sitting in the cave a teacher
> showing girls how to defuse bombs
> it's squatting in the bunker a mother
> giving the little one her breast between shifts
>
> it lives under ground
> not on the earth

The Vietnam War brought the sufferings of people in the "Third World" into full view and consciousness, but people also became aware of the courage, strength and hope of the liberation movements. Another poem, "Different Answers," speaks of Dorothee's various encounters with the people in the destroyed land of Vietnam. The traveler's opening query elicits songs and tales of bomb victims' struggles and suffering; the poem concludes with the "bomb-proof" truth, the hope of the liberation movements.

Everywhere we ask
if it will come tomorrow
or in the spring
or in the spring after that
peace

pham van dong the president of the liberated people
breaks out in uproarious laughter
against the tiny ray of hope for today and tomorrow
that has just been bombed to smithereens again

he sets the truth
simple and bomb-proof
"on n'arrete pas le soleil"

you can't stop the sun.[3]

For Dorothee Soelle, Vietnam became a symbol for the cross, and at the same time for resurrection. "I thought that I had known what it meant when I said, 'I am a Christian.' In those words I expressed a relationship to a human being who lived two thousand years ago and who spoke the truth. I tried to take that man seriously, because I believed that his story has implications to this very day. I could find no difference worth mentioning between a crown of thorns and these tear-gas derivatives that, under unfavorable wind conditions, cause you not only to cry and vomit, but also to suffocate. I could find no difference worth mentioning between the newly tested shells and poisons and the ancient technique of killing people by crucifixion. The Vietnam War did two things for my generation: Like nothing before, it unmasked capitalism. And, at the same time, the Vietnamese people—representative of other peoples—gave us the gift of a new vision of life, of the future."[4]

A focal message of the Political Evensong became the discovery that the Crucified One could be found in Vietnam, that He was not ensconced in the sacred space of the churches. This was an insight that permeated broad segments of Christianity worldwide. Along with the realization of the human rights violations in Vietnam came a fundamental expansion of perspectives. No longer was the sole focus on the burden of guilt toward the victims of the past; now there was also the feeling of responsibility for the current "wretched of the earth."[5] The Western superpower was now stomping on its own declaration of liberty and human rights in order to secure its strategic interests in one of the poorest countries on earth. People thus also began to pay attention to what the United States was doing in the other countries of Asia, Africa and Latin America. The crusading ideology of the West, forever claiming to fight Communism, was increasingly unmasking itself as a cruel strategy of deception.

It had first come to public attention in 1969 in ecumenical circles, at the World Council of Churches conference in Uppsala, Sweden, that the structures of the global market are quite deadly. The WCC challenged Christians to change their ways, especially in the wealthy countries of Europe and North America. This was also the time when the "Theology of Liberation" that was emerging in Latin America was bringing about a radical shift in perspective. Julia Esquivel,[6] the Guatemalan theologian whom Dorothee admired, wrote: "God wanted to reveal God's son in the 'wretched of the earth.'[7] And in their misery we comprehended God's misery, and in their broken sobs we shared God's tears. And their lament upset the calm of our life and brought new life to the roots of our faith. And we awoke to the life of truth that is called crisis, conflict and the path of hope."[8]

Vietnam

They've stopped bombing
and coming in low over their targets
swords have still not been made into sickles[9]

The Crucified One was also to be found in Vietnam, not ensconced in the churches' sacred spaces. This thought became a core message of the Political Evensong. The poster announcing the theme for the February 6–7, 1973, Evensong reads: "Vietnam and its Accomplices."

Jetzt haben sie aufgehört
zu bombn und im Tiefflug zu ziehen
Noch sind die Schwerter nicht zu Sicheln ~~um~~gesc
miedet

Aber die B 52 stehen still.
Wir lachen und weinen
Te Deum laudamus,so snagen die Väter
Sollen wir nicht noch ein Kind machen
sagt mir mein Mann.

Ich sehe den petit lac in Hanoi
Zwischen den Trümmern ~~gehen~~ suchen die Menschen
Hinter der Pagode steigt der Mond auf
Aus den Lautsprechern klingt Musik
und die Leute sehe ich
lachen
weinen
~~sich küssen~~ zärtlich gehen

Ja ,sage ich ihnen
Das ist ein Grund
zum Kinderzeugen.

Facsimile of poem manuscript with Soelle's handwritten corrections

but the B52s are grounded
we laugh and cry
te deum laudamus our fathers sang
how about making another baby
my husband says to me

I see the *petit lac* in hanoi
people picking through the rubble
the moon rises behind the pagoda
the loudspeakers play music
and I see the people
laughing
crying
walking arm in arm

Yes, I say to them
good reason
for making babies.[10]

In the encounters with those who live on the periphery of poverty, Biblical texts were also read in a new way. It became clear that the essential legacies and messages of both testaments originated not in the centers of power, but in the shacks of foreign workers in the shadow of the mega-cultures' prestigious projects. And the murdered and resurrected Messiah suddenly became identical with the tortured victims of military dictatorships and the death squadrons. But he also came to symbolize the suffering and the strength of the weak. Ernesto Cardenal, Nicaraguan priest, poet and activist, wrote in a long documentary poem to Monsignor Casaldàliga, the "father" of the indigenous people of the Amazon who are threatened with extinction: "We know only this: wherever the helicopters circle, there is the body of Christ."[11]

With this insight, many Christians of both Protestant and Catholic confessions became more committed to political and economic justice. In 1965 in Columbia, Camilo Torres, priest and sociologist, became the spokesperson for a mass movement against poverty and violence. "Revolution is a Commandment for Christians," he said as early as 1964 at the Catholic Pastoral Conference "Pro Mundi Vita" in Leuwen, Belgium. "Why do the Christians argue with the Communists about whether the soul is mortal or immortal when we know that hunger is fatal?"[12] At this same time in the mid-1960s, Ernesto Cardenal was spending time in Columbia and wrote his *Psalms of Struggle and Liberation* there.[13]

Listen to My Just Cause Lord: Psalm 16

Listen to my just cause Lord
be attentive to my cry
You who are the defender of the disappeared
And of those condemned in the councils of war
free me from the dictator
and from the mafia of gangsters.
Their machine guns are set up against us
And their hate slogans surround us
Spies surround my house
The secret police watch me at night
I am in the midst of gangsters
Arise Lord
    come to meet them
        defeat them,

Snatch me from the claws of the banks,
with your hand, Lord, free me from the businessmen
and the elite club members.
We are not allowed in their club,
but you will satisfy our hunger
when night comes

Christians in the solidarity movements of the 1960s increasingly recognized the importance of God's partisanship as protector of the weak. They understood the indestructible link between the "option for the poor" and the biblical message. Indeed, this option was impressively affirmed by the Latin American Bishops' Conference in 1968 in Medellín, Columbia, where the entire ecumenical world was set into motion politically and theologically. The World Council of Churches established its Anti-Racism Program, thereby deciding to support the liberation movements in southern Africa. Grass-roots Christian movements in many countries participated in reform and liberation movements.

Dorothee and her friends were connected in many different ways with these movements, and this, too, would continue to transform her theological thinking. In 1971 her second important book, *Political Theology: A Critical Reflection on the Theology of Rudolf Bultmann,* was published. During her student years, Bultmann's rationally based project of demythologizing the gospel had provided Soelle an important way to gain access to the Bible and to theology. Now she sought to define the line that she had crossed over, through political praxis and the analysis of political praxis: "Bultmann . . . thinks within the confines of a bourgeois understanding of scholarship as objective and unrelated to the times."[14] Pointing to the way consumers in Western countries were implicated in the misery of workers on the banana and coffee plantations in Latin America, she wanted with this book to put the personal concept of sin into a structural, economic context.

Bultmann, who knew and respected Soelle, wrote her a thoughtfully formulated four-page letter. He argued: "There is a difference, surely, between killing or robbing a banana worker and getting my bananas through the United Fruit Company. If the banana worker is paid a pittance for his labor, he always has the option of striking or going to court."[15]

Those who had learned from Political Evensong's actions, from information, analysis and discussion, to recognize the reasons for poverty and violence and the contexts in which they occur, could no longer think according to Bultmann's logic as expressed in his response to Soelle's political theology. It became increasingly clear that the church as well as theological scholarship must occupy themselves with politics, economics and sociology. Related to this was social-critical analysis, which for many led to active political involvement based on reality as they experienced or perceived it. The movement "Christians for Socialism" had its beginnings at this time and Dorothee became actively involved in it. She was very concrete in describing its goals: "If you ask, 'Does one become a Christian for Socialism?' Then I would answer: Love your neighbor and notice what you experience in doing so. . . . The more you open yourself to your neighbor, the more you have to be concerned about the world your neighbor lives in; their housing, work and socialization, their overall life situation. The truly merciful person will in any case bite granite some day—that is, the structures of ownership and social class."[16]

The movement for social justice appealed especially to the youth in Western societies. The student movements and the social movements beginning around 1968 transformed personal goals and interpersonal relationships as well as social institutions. Naturally the churches were transformed as well. The emerging anti-war movement could not be overlooked, especially in the United States itself. Young men refused military service, burned their draft cards and risked long prison sentences. Injured war veterans returning from Vietnam demonstrated on crutches and in wheelchairs against the continuation of the war. In the summer of 1975, after ten years, the war ended with the conquest of Saigon by the liberation army of the Viet Cong. Not long after that, a friend of peace in the United States looked up Dorothee after a lecture and asked for her signature on his

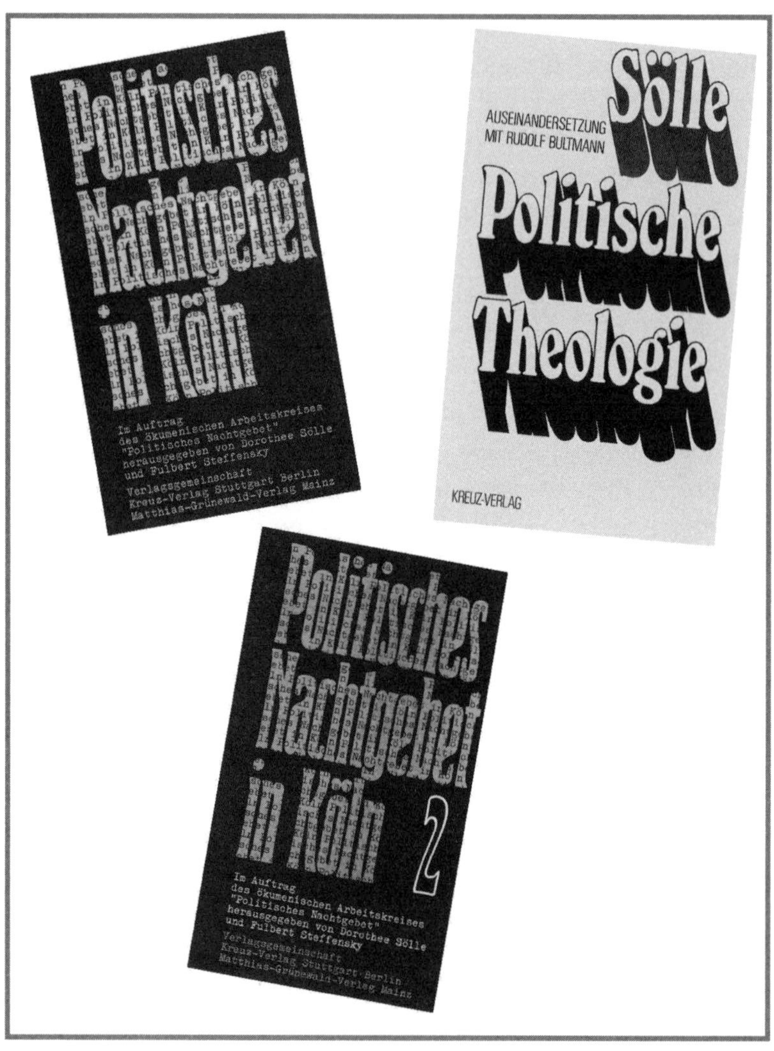

Three major books by Dorothee Soelle are published between 1969 and 1971: Two volumes of texts from the Political Evensong, and her Political Theology, *a critique of Rudolf Bultmann.*

Prof. D. Rudolf Bultmann
355 Marburg (Lahn)
Calvinstraße 14

Marburg, 7.-14. Aug. 1971

Tel. 25265

An Frau Dr. Dorothee Sölle

Verehrte u. liebe Frau Sölle!

Für Ihren freundlichen Brief vom 15. Juli und für die Übersendung der „Politischen Theologie", die Ihre Auseinandersetzung mit mir enthält, danke ich Ihnen herzlich. Da ich nicht mehr lesen kann, habe ich mir das 5. Kapitel u. auch die Kapp. 7 u. 8 vorlesen lassen. Ich bin nun infolge meines Alters und meines angegriffenen Befindens nicht im Stande, mich ausführlich mit Ihnen auseinander zu setzen, sondern muß mich auf knappe Bemerkungen beschränken, und das mit dem Vorbehalt, daß ich Ihr Buch noch nicht vollständig kennen gelernt habe.

Wohl nehme ich einen Zusammenhang zwischen Ihrer „politischen Theologie" und meiner theologischen Arbeit wahr, aber auch einen entscheidenden Unterschied, ja auch Gegensatz. Der Gegensatz besteht offenbar vor allem darin, daß ich von dem dialektischen Verhältnis zwischen einer jenseitigen, transzendenten Wirklichkeit [und der innerweltlichen Wirklichkeit] rede, während Sie nur die innerweltliche Wirklichkeit gelten lassen. Ihr Verständnis des Glaubens als Entweltlichung ist orientiert am „Vorverständnis der Schicksalhaftigkeit der Zustände und Ordnungen" (S. 79). Im Gegenteil! er ist gerade unabhängig von diesen, ohne daß er „die Preisgabe der sozialen politischen Vernunft, die die Welt für veränderbar hält" (S. 79). Das Gegenteil ist der Fall: der Glaube gibt die Freiheit zur Veränderung der Welt. Es gilt: δός μοι ποῦ στῶ, καὶ κινήσω τὴν γῆν.

Ich bin also ganz darin mit Ihnen einverstanden, daß Sie fordern, daß die Theologie Theorie und Praxis zu vermitteln habe (S. 105). Aber dazu bedarf es nicht einer „politischen" Theologie, sondern es ist die Aufgabe der Theologie überhaupt, sofern sie die Strukturen der gegenwärtigen ... die Verantwortung des Glaubens für die Strukturen der gegenwärtigen

Facsimile first page of Rudolf Bultmann's letter to Dorothee Soelle regarding her book, Political Theology *(1971)*

copy of her poem about the mayor of Hanoi,[17] which he especially loved:

The Mayor of Hanoi

The mayor of hanoi
nearly bald his face all wrinkles
claims
he's only twenty-seven
he bases that claim
on the age of the republic
ho chi minh taught the citizens
all to be the same age
as old as the cause they love

According to this arithmetic
the mayor's grandchildren
are already twenty-seven
and later people will live
as old books promise
a thousand years and more

10

Suffering and Passion

"The only way one can really grow into Christ is to grow into the movement for resistance."—Dorothee Soelle

There is no alien suffering!"[1] This statement is heard often in the context of the movements for social change that brought countless people into the streets from the late

1960s onward. "Everything that happens is your business," the poet Günther Eich[2] called out to the Easter March demonstrators. Thanks to the media, the entire world had become more visible; everyone could see what was happening in Vietnam, South Africa, Prague or Santiago de Chile. "No one is an island," said Martin Luther King, and Robert Kennedy took up this motto as a candidate for President of the United States in 1968. Robert Kennedy embodied the American hope for change, for the end of the war in Vietnam, for the rejection of the imperialist form of the *American dream* in favor of a *just and compassionate society—to make gentle the life in this world.* This dream of the "other America" ended abruptly with the assassinations of both Martin Luther King and Robert Kennedy in April and November 1967, respectively. What remained was their vision of a new kind of human cooperation characterized by the capacity for *compassion.*

The concept of *com-passio*, the capacity to suffer *with* another, became a central focus for Dorothee Soelle at this time as well. For even if it was unthinkable to "stop the sun," victories and progress in the struggle for justice were necessarily associated with victims, whose suffering one had not only to mourn, but to share. Indeed, people in these movements again and again experienced at an existential level the many diverse actions that they took out of solidarity with victims of oppression, violence, and suffering. Dorothee, herself involved in the solidarity movements for Latin America and in the grassroots communities of these countries, wrote in retrospect:

> The Theology of Liberation taught me to understand the Bible not only as a call to do God's will in a world of injustice, but even as the call to accept discrimination, hardships and martyrdom as part of the bargain. "Whoever wants to hold on to life shall lose it" means that to follow the way of resistance in faith is to consciously take this risk. . . . We must resist the way the foundations of our life are being destroyed, the poor

> are being left at Death's door, and a so-called "peace" is being constructed based on the reign of madness. The only way to become a Christian and grow into Christ is to grow into a movement of resistance.[3]

The struggles and hard times of that period were reflected in many ways in Dorothee Soelle's texts from that period. They remind one that these times were infused with great hope for change, with revolutionary enthusiasm and willingness to sacrifice. But they also call to mind how much violence was perpetrated to persecute and destroy the Latin American liberation movements. On September 11, 1973, the Chilean Air Force bombed La Moneda, the presidential palace and Chilean government headquarters of the democratically elected socialist president Salvador Allende. He was the first president of a democratically elected Popular Front government made up of socialists and communists to also be supported by a small Christian Socialist Party. Its policy of radical social reforms was the declared target of attacks by the United States and by multinational corporations. Allende's government was violently overthrown in a collaborative action by the various secret services and the Chilean military. President Allende, who was offered safe passage from La Moneda and from the country if he would resign from office, turned to the public as he left the burning presidential palace and called over the last free radio station:[4]

> My fellow Chileans, My friends! Surely this will be the last opportunity for me to address you. The Air Force has bombed the broadcast facilities of Radio Magallanes. . . . Given these facts I can say only one thing to the working people: I am not going to resign! Placed into a historic transition, I will pay for loyalty to the people with my life. And I say to them that I am certain that the seeds that we have planted in the good conscience of thousands and thousands of Chileans will not be shriveled forever. They have force and will be able to

> dominate us, but social processes can be arrested neither by crime nor by force. . . . Workers of my homeland! I want to thank you for the loyalty that you always had, the confidence that you placed in a man who was only an interpreter of your great yearnings for justice, who gave his word that he would respect the Constitution and the law and did just that. Others will overcome this dark and bitter moment when treason seeks to prevail. Go forward, knowing that sooner rather than later, the avenues will be opened again on which free human beings shall walk to construct a better society. Long live Chile! Long live the people! Long live the workers! These are my last words, and I am certain that my sacrifice will not be in vain.

The Chilean revolution had been nonviolent. However, after the fall of the Allende government, conflicts on the Latin American continent became more militant and more violent. At the same time, theologians and bishops sided more and more clearly with the Theology of Liberation, and base communities sprang up everywhere, professing their solidarity with the poor and declaring the necessity for social change. Soon they were targeted ideologically and politically by conservative forces in both church and society. Dom Helder Camara, Roman Catholic Bishop of Brazil at this time, minced no words: "When I feed the poor they call me a saint. When I ask why so many people are poor they call me a communist."[5] The liberation churches supported social movements, the occupation of land, and human rights groups—and soon they themselves had thousands of martyrs to mourn.

The fate of the church of martyrs in El Salvador and of its bishop, Oscar Arnulfo Romero, the "dirty war" in Columbia and Guatemala, all found expression in Dorothee's poems, newspaper reports and saints' legends, which she used to give shape to her sense of connectedness with the people of that continent. In these texts, the suffering and crucified Christ becomes manifest in a new way. At the same time Dorothee developed her Christology to a new stage of equal importance to her Christology of "Christ the Representative," namely the Christology of solidarity. Here, Christ is not merely the one who shares compassionately in people's suffering; rather Christ himself needs and hopes for human solidarity with his own suffering. Discipleship is redefined by human solidarity with the suffering

CHILE

Hoffnung im Widerstand

Politisches Nachtgebet am 10.9. 18 Uhr in St. Katharinen

Christen für den Sozialismus
- Hamburg -

Image of Evensong Program: Chile—Hope in Resistance: The Movement "Christians for Socialism," to which Dorothee Soelle also belongs, reacts to the military putsch in Chile by organizing a Political Evensong in Hamburg.

Christ. Dietrich Bonhoeffer had already written in a similar situation of resisting and suffering from his Tegel prison cell in Berlin:

> "Could you not stay awake with me one hour?' Jesus asks in Gethsemane (Matt.26:40b). That is the opposite of everything a religious person expects from God. The human being is called upon to share in God's suffering at the hands of a godless world. Thus we must live in that godless world and not try to cover up or transfigure its godlessness somehow with religion. . . . It is not a religious act that makes someone a Christian, but rather sharing in God's suffering in the worldly life."[6]

"Being with Christ in Gethsemane" becomes the archetype of compassion. When the young German social worker Elisabeth Käsemann,[7] like thousands of others fighting the abuses of Argentinian dictator Augusto Pinochet, disappeared in the torture centers of the military junta in 1977 and died a miserable death, Dorothee Soelle wrote the poem "Report from Argentina:"[8]

D says it's a rule in the underground
to say nothing for two days when being tortured[9]
that gives the comrades time
two days I ask does that also mean two nights
Yes, she says they work shifts

O God I say when I'm alone
in case you're able to remember
go to those being tortured
make them strong
and have mercy on those
who talk sooner

O Jesus I say when we're together
You were tortured thursday and friday

You didn't betray any names
You preferred to die

You did not use
the supertechnology of supergod
otherwise all of our names would have been betrayed
and power still almighty
and technology still supertechnology.

D says
it's a rule in the underground
to say nothing for two days when being tortured
and what do we do I ask myself
two days and two nights in gethsemane
and what
do we do

In these dramatic years Dorothee's book *Suffering* appeared in the series Themes in Theology. It is one of her most succinct and most important books. In it she posits the question of the existence of God in suffering. At the same time she explores an interpretation of the traditional concept of passion, not merely as passive suffering, but as active, passionate engagement. This leads her to recognize Christ's passion not as an expiatory sacrifice, but as an act of passionate devotion. Referring to the Christology of the Gospel of John, according to which God appears, works, and suffers in the person of Christ, Soelle calls the crucified Christ the symbol of the love of God who is prepared to undergo suffering, who even becomes powerless and in need of human help. Here, too, Soelle takes up ideas of Bonhoeffer:[10] "The same God who is with us is the God who forsakes us. . . . Before God, and with God, we live without God. God consents to be pushed out of the world and onto the cross; God is weak and powerless in the world and in precisely this way, and only so, is at our side and helps us. . . . This is the crucial distinction between Christianity and all religions. Human religiosity directs people in need to the power of God in the world, God as *deus ex machina*. The Bible directs people toward the powerlessness and suffering of God."

Soelle further develops the related idea of human maturity (*Mündigkeit*) and the capacity of human beings to participate actively in the suffering of God and God's creatures. In the tradition of early Reformation theologian Thomas Müntzer, she distinguishes the "martyrs of God," whose sufferings serve life, from the "martyrs of the devil," who devotedly accept the violent conditions imposed by whatever regime is in power. She continues:[11]

> If the most important question addressed to suffering is whom it serves, God or the devil, becoming alive or paralysis, passion for life or the destruction of this passion, then the other question addressed to suffering, namely, that of theodicy, appears to be superseded. The almighty Lord, who ordains suffering or frees one from it has in that case lost his all-surpassing significance. Whoever grounds suffering in an almighty, alien One who ordains everything, has to face the question of the justice of this God—and must be shattered by it. . . . People who are shattered by this God, experienced as heteronomous, who allows evil as if he were possessed by our baser instincts, are people who think too much of God and too little of themselves.

Soelle seeks the passion of Jesus as present in ever-new ways when people voluntarily take suffering upon themselves for a just cause. She compares Jesus' farewell words in the Gospel of John with the farewell letters written to loved ones by those in the European resistance to Hitler after being sentenced to death. In her eyes the statements of these men and women, in many cases communists, are on a level with Jesus' consciousness:[12]

Freedom from fear, certainty, strength mark these letters. They grow out of participating in a cause that is greater than the people who work for it and die in the process . . . [H]ow the man Jesus suffered means a strengthening, a presentation of human possibilities, a hope of humanizing even our suffering. . . . Jesus' passion is the quintessence of such freely chosen suffering. It is suffering at the hands of the 'world,' of society that refuses to acknowledge Jesus's claims. It is also passion in the modern sense, passionate commitment to the unconditional. . . . By its nature, suffering hits us in such a way that it makes us "the devil's martyrs." Fear, speechlessness, aggression, and blind hate are confirmed and spread through suffering. In Christ, that is, in humanity's true possibility, which is by no means self-evident, suffering summons our self-confidence, our boldness, our strength. Our oneness with love is indissoluble. To learn to suffer without becoming the devil's martyrs means to live conscious of our oneness with the whole of life. Those who suffer in this way are indestructible. Nothing can separate them from the love of God.

For Julia Esquivel[13]

In the park I read your poems Julia
and sigh when you speak of the quetzal
who lost all language the indios say
when the spaniards invaded the land
the tropical bird I'd like to see once
in the time I'm still here

And shake my head in annoyance
when you never tire of calling out
the names of the murdered peoples
and the locations of the massacres
confusing poetry

with geography
julia, bird of beautiful colors
whom I have never seen
in the time I've been here

Oh well am I doing anything differently
saying buchenwald and terezin[14] again and again
words like lidice[15] that no one wants to hear
adding mutlangen[16] into the mix
and greenham common[17]
like you I call to the quetzal julia
whom I'd like to see once
in the time I'm still here[18]

11

Journey

In the spring of 1975 Dorothee spent four weeks in a simple house in Cinqueterre, Italy, writing "texts and reflections on religious experience." Presumably the purpose of this retreat was to give her the chance to probe the question of her own mid-life identity. She could look back on exciting, but stressful years of change, both in her personal life and in the political sphere—from the Political Evensong and the emergence of the "Christians for Socialism" movement to the struggles and conflicts with the conservative authorities in churches and universities alike. What moved her at this stage is summarized in the brief prologue to the book she called *Hinreise* (Journey):[1]

> "Travel" is an ancient image for the experiences of the soul on its journey to the self. The journey one begins in meditation and contemplative reflection is religion's way of helping people find their way to their own identity. Christian faith puts an emphasis on the "journey back" into the world and its responsibilities. But faith requires a deeper certainty than what we obtain through action. That is what the "journey" is about.[2]

Once again Dorothee returned to her primal fears and longings, to the beginning of the great search that had led her to study theology: "I was not 'religious.' I had no prayer life, no relationship to any particular supernatural being and no connection whatsoever to the church. I simply wanted to know 'the truth.' I had not found it in philosophy—at least not in ways tangible or practical enough to meet my needs. It was my sense of things that I couldn't spend my life doing nothing but working and consuming things; my life should have a direction . . . If I try to put this undefined wish into words, this is what occurs to me:

To be whole, not to live a fragmented life
To be whole, not to be destroyed
To make whole, not to break
To hunger for justice, not to feel satisfied in the face of injustice
To live authentically, not unconsciously-apathetically
To get to Heaven, not to remain in Hell."[3]

To feel satisfied, complacent, in the presence of injustice—that is the "death by bread alone" that provides the title of the English version of Dorothee's *Hinreise.* Contempt for oneself and alienation are godlessness; authentic life is to be whole, "not later" or "over on the other side," but "here and now." By now Dorothee was aware that in order to overcome alienation and fragmentation, one must take the political and economic conditions that contributed to them into account. But she had become suspicious of political activism. True and necessary action in the world, too, required a spiritual dimension. She had always been interested in the mystics; now they became increasingly important to her. On March 31, 1974 she wrote Luise Schottroff from Italy:

Dear Luise, you dear old dreadful creature!

I dreamed about you last night and you said in a quiet but energetic voice: "You can't do it that way!" You had your hair

> piled high in a toupée and a bit of your scalp was showing on the side. What this is supposed to mean I don't know, except maybe that your hair is standing on end in disgust?
>
> I find myself taking mystical detours. Perhaps I've read too much of the stuff and have become intoxicated by the 'sweetness of God,' but the materialist aspect of Marxism seems so stupid to me at the moment, so small-minded and capable of leading to erroneous conclusions (which it certainly does in the un-dialectical form we see for the most part!), and the 'inner world' of religion, of myth, so appealing. You were probably scolding me for all this in the dream. . . . I'm sitting here on my terrace, before me the ocean, behind me the vineyards, above them the sun that's a bit clouded over today. I have knit together this religion lecture with a few gaps remaining. I wish nothing more than that you could be here to hear me give it, too.[4]

By then—and until the end of Dorothee's life—Luise Schottroff and Dorothee Soelle were each other's "best friend." They shared essential interests and experiences. Both were women theologians who were politically engaged; both were women scholars who managed to combine profession and family. Both had experienced opposition and enmity and encountered obstacles. And both had husbands who supported them in their work and in their public debates and controversies. From the beginning they had a way of life that for most women really only became possible to live out a generation later; now they supported each other in this unusual life experiment. The two couples visited each other often and without the usual formalities, exchanged ideas about alternative lifestyles and child-rearing, and were at home in the same theological and political circles.

Growing up near Berlin as the daughter of a pastor in the tradition of the Confessing Church, Luise came from a completely different world. She brought a totally different tone into their discussions. Dorothee characterized Luise in her memoir: "The teacher of New Testament and feminist liberation theologian helped me learn to read the Bible with rigor and enthusiasm. . . . She laughed with me when the men strutted about all too arrogantly; she cried with me when the fish were dying in the Rhine. Her Prussian realism looks with some indignation on my spiritual excursions, and my Rhenish joie de vivre tickles her suspicious nature. Her perseverance has again and again renewed my rootedness in this land of our mothers."[5]

Luise Schottroff is an exegete; she got Dorothee to take biblical texts seriously, to read them more rigorously and to interpret them critically rather than simply using them to flesh out her theological and philosophical ideas. Dorothee Soelle was at home in systematic theology; she thought more in philosophical and psychological categories, while also exploring mysticism. Luise said of her: "She made it possible for me to be not only a theologian, but a Christian, in the sense of 'we are (also, and in a different way) church.'"[6] Luise, the precise biblical exegete and Dorothee, the thinker whose mental acrobatics took flight, complemented each other perfectly in their theological work. Their collaborative bible studies and coauthored books[7] had achieved a level of theological education and community-building work that extended far beyond local congregations and church denominations.

So Dorothee now sat on the Mediterranean shore and wrote Luise—who actually felt more of a pull toward the North Sea—telling her what she was up to. She was reading *Das Büchlein der ewigen Weisheit* (The Little Book of Eternal Wisdom) by the medieval Dominican mystic Heinrich Seuse (Henry Suso) and found in it a kind of "practical, non-speculative wisdom, guidelines in matters of faith and conduct."[8] In the search for inner healing and wholeness she discovered that identity cannot be achieved one-sidedly through work, action or effort. "To become at one with oneself means here to transcend the 'self' as something that is already there. . . . To gain one's identity means to transcend this ego."[9] But this is only possible by submitting oneself to a transcendent world and power, to the reality of God. She offered Psalm 139 as an example for this life path: "O Lord, you have searched me and known me . . . Search me, O God, and know my heart."

> The 139th Psalm speaks directly to the matter of the identity of a human being. It is an answer to the questions: Who am I? What am I looking for in this world? Where am I headed? Where do I come from? What does my being here mean?
>
> . . . I do not live by my own strength; I am not autonomous; I am dependent. Of myself I would have no life worthy of the name, but with God I have life. But what does that word "God" mean here? It is probably a good idea at this point to think back to what the mystics called "letting go of oneself" and "letting oneself sink." Clearly the psalmist praying this psalm did indeed let himself go, let himself sink into the uttermost depths; yet he is actually borne and upheld, completely surrounded and enveloped, by God. . . . .
>
> Who am I? The answer is: God knows me better than I know myself, differently from the way those around me know me, longer and deeper than any who know anything about me. That means that my identity is more, can be more, than that which is already known about me. Scripture (1 John 3:2) puts it this way: 'And what we shall be has not yet been revealed.'[10] It means that every human being is a mystery that is not swallowed up into social identity. Every human being is a mystery, something I understand only in union with God. To love means not only to discover the other. It also means to realize the other in their boundless depth, their indestructibility, precisely as they are known by God.[11]

It was at this time that Dorothee wrote "A Poem about the ice age/about psalm fifty-one/about the little mermaid/and about you"[12]

Dorothee Soelle was one of the most highly regarded theologians of her time, yet in her lifetime she never received a university teaching appointment in Germany.

and gave it to her husband for his birthday. Among other things it reflects, in what can be assumed to be a code for her own mid-life crisis, her question: Who am I and where is my life heading? The family had just moved to Hamburg; the two older children were leaving the nest. Fulbert had accepted a Professorship of Education in Religious Studies at the University of Hamburg. This city would be their new home, but Dorothee felt like a stranger there, at least at the beginning.

She had no local work-related connections. She applied for a teaching contract at the University of Bremen, but was turned down. Her meditation on Psalm 51 ("Create in me a clean heart, O God, and put a new and right spirit within me") was nothing more than a longing for a heart free from fear and for the "acre of land we still need," for the warmth of an unbreakable bond and an earth that felt like home.

A poem about the ice age/about psalm fifty-one/
about the little mermaid/and about you

Create in me a different heart god
warmer than the ice age
give me the strength to swim
now that I've dived in to the pool
borne I think I could bear more
I would like my clarity to grow
but what grows every day
is only my fear for you
allied with my fear of you
. . . .

I would like my warmth to grow
but what grows every day
is my fear of you
always when winter came again
it lay as if between us
the sun did not speak to the earth
the earth hid all it had
it didn't even unfold the ferns
and didn't know where to put the little white
flowers or the swamp-golden ones
you can't come out she said
he'll beat you to death she said
there's nothing funny about it she said

Create in me a heart without fear god
and while you're at it give me new feet
I don't want to walk on a thousand knives
the stumbling the beating down the bleeding
I don't want to keep only trying to avoid
instead of swimming straight ahead as before
with the arrow-straight whip of my back fin

. . . .

Create in me new feet god
the new walk

Create in me a heart without fear god
didn't the earth stay there during the ice age
though it could have emigrated too
it stayed it waited

I would like my love to grow
like the earth under the ice
that moves and remains there
that pulls back and becomes small
and remains
longer than any winter

I'd like to sing with you again
not only listen or forget myself in sounds
I'd like to have memory together with you
and the acre of land we still need

It gets colder when you eat alone
when you drink alone
when you cover yourself
with mourning

Create in me the earth god[13]

12

Leaving My Mother's Home and My Father's Country

In the summer of 1974, a group of "scouts" from the United States traveled around the Federal Republic of Germany. Comprised of professors and students of Union Theological Seminary in New York, their assignment was to make inquiries about prospective candidates for a professorship at Union Seminary. At that time, the number of qualified women available for such a position was still small. Beverly Harrison, the first woman professor at the Seminary, had proposed that the noted and controversial German theologian Dorothee Soelle be called to Union Theological Seminary as a visiting professor. But before contacting her directly, of course, they wanted to gather information about her. The "scouts" met with representatives of churches and universities and returned with the report that "Dorothee Soelle will never get a professorship in Germany, but all theologians, female and male, are reading her!"[1] So Dorothee seemed to be just the right person for Union!

Tom Driver, Professor of Theology and Literature at Union at that time, took part in this exploratory trip; he also remembers subsequent conversations with Dorothee Soelle and her family. There was an agreement between Union and Professor Soelle prior to her appointment that she would teach for one probationary year, living in New York with her husband and children. After that first year they would see about continuing the appointment or not. All of Union was curious to meet this visiting professor with such an interesting public image. She was said to be political and religious—but hopefully not all too religious!

Union Theological Seminary in New York, founded in 1836, soon became a leading center of liberal theology in the United States. Seminaries in the United States are part of the second phase of theological education. Students live and study there after completing an undergraduate college or university degree. Thus many students at Union are older; some have already worked in other professions or have other educational backgrounds. Some are teachers or taxi drivers, catechists or social workers; some are women who have interrupted their career path for the sake of family. There are guests from the ecumenical world, scholars from Europe or other continents who hold fellowships. They come from various regions and churches, have had diverse social experiences and religious upbringing, but they all share a common goal: They want to practice their Christian faith in the context of the world in which they live and take on faith-based responsibilities.

Accordingly, theological social ethics is one of the key focal points of Union Theological Seminary. Reinhold Niebuhr, among the best-known theologians at Union, was instrumental in developing Christian social ethics and was strongly indebted to the American tradition of the Social Gospel, developed by Walter Rauschenbusch and others. The Social Gospel tradition maintained that the biblical commandments are meant not only for instruction in conduct of the individual in Christian life but that they must also translate into social and political categories and contexts. For social ethics, engaging in dialogue with modern cultural and social sciences was just as indispensable for this process of transfer to social and political categories and contexts as the interpretation and actualization of biblical texts. This position fundamentally distinguished Union from the personal piety of mainstream Protestant Evangelicalism and Fundamentalism in the United States as well as from the conservative Lutheran tradition that was alive and well at the time in Germany, which separated faith from politics. Dietrich Bonhoeffer, too, Niebuhr's most famous student, held to that Lutheran tradition for a time, until he became "converted" during his year of study at Union to a new perspective on the Bible and the practice of faith.

Dorothee needed no such conversion. As a matter of fact, she was actually quite devout, but in an unconventional way. She fit perfectly into the Union scene—and that is where she went. She lived with Fulbert and their daughters Mirjam and Caroline for one year in McGiffert Hall at Union Seminary, the venerable residential complex for professors and other Seminary employees. The neo-Gothic structure of Union lies directly across the upper Broadway on the grounds of Columbia University but also in the immediate neighborhood of Harlem, the well-known black community. Dorothee was thrilled with New York and her work at the seminary. Her way of life, her teaching style and her political theology had made her the target of non-stop attacks in Germany; here, by contrast, she fit right in. When her husband was called to a position at the University of Hamburg, she decided to stay in New York—at least for half the time. Union was keen to keep her and agreed to continue this arrangement. For the next ten years she would teach there during each spring term and return to her family in Hamburg for the six months of fall and winter.

The separation was difficult for all concerned, but for Dorothee it was nevertheless a stroke of good fortune and very gratifying. "She really blossomed during that time," recalls daughter Mirjam Steffensky. Dorothee was apparently not only one to have discovered happiness by beginning something new in mid-life, by being somewhere quite new and different, by teaching as it came naturally to her, fully engaged and with emotion, without being subjected to threats and attacks. Students and companions on her journey of those years also look back and tell of sharing a happy and inspiring experience.

"She had a great thirst for life," says Tom Driver, adding that he knew no one else who loved life like Dorothee. At Union, team teaching was already taken for granted; her first team-taught seminar on theology and literature dealt with Bertolt Brecht. Her speeches and lectures made abundant use of poetry, points out Tom Driver; it was "theopoetics."[2] Theology professors in Germany were totally helpless to know what to do with that concept.

Janet Walton, Professor of Worship and the Arts, says: "She was devout as well as militant." The two women were at one in their love of music and the arts, but also in their investment in creating worship services that took place every weekday at noon during the academic year at Union. Dorothee missed hardly any of these services, helped plan them and often presented the meditation. Janet also remembers Dorothee lovingly and with admiration: "What a woman she was!" In her book *Art and Worship: A Vital Connection*, she wrote that Dorothee brought with her a beauty that is needed today in the church, and yet at the same time she was unrelenting when it came to exposing the injustice and greed of the Western economic order. That unrelenting manner often left her hearers speechless, but also challenged them to respond.[3]

One of Dorothee's first meditations was called "Leaving my mother's home and my father's country." There, in New York, far away from her place of origin, the search for home was once again her theme. She has moved away from her country, her church, and her family of origin—Was there a place she could call home?

There are indications that Union Seminary and New York City became such a place for her for the next few years. People from different countries and cultures come together there; the neighborhood of upper Broadway alone offers a rich palette of diverse cultural experiences. Where else does one find the concert hall of the New York

Philharmonic Orchestra next to bars and cafes like those Dorothee found at the time, like the Cuban Jazz Bar and the Café Nussbaum & Wu?

Dorothee could not get enough of the concerts and exhibits, movies or theatre, nor of the numerous political and cultural activities of the American grassroots movements. Soon she was attending every kind of event and forging ties to every social movement and

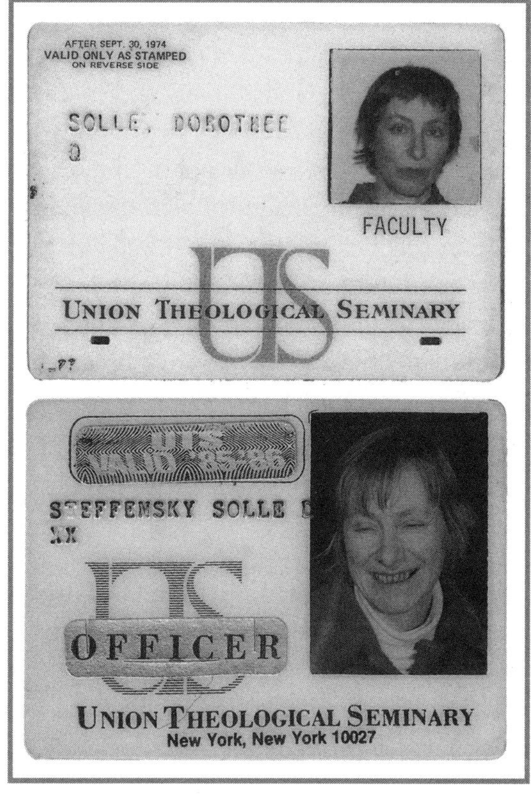

Two Union Seminary Faculty ID *cards document the beginning and the end of Dorothee Soelle's twelve-year university career in the United States.*

its activists. At the same time she was in close contact with her students and colleagues, both men and women, engaging in scholarly exchange with them. The atmosphere she helped create, and experienced, at Union in the 1970s and 1980s came alive again when many of them gathered in the fall of 2003 for a memorial celebration *In Memory of Dorothee Soelle* at the annual conference of the American Academy of Religion in Atlanta. In their remembrances speakers recalled the militant protest movements against the conservative America of Presidents Nixon and Reagan, the calls for and actions of solidarity with Latin American liberation movements, the merging of old civil rights and peace movements with the new social movements of feminists, gays, and lesbians, and of Greenpeace activists. And in the midst of it all, Dorothee Soelle, hungry for life, pugnacious, engaged everywhere, was always in motion. Her colleague and friend Beverly Harrison concluded with the weighty summary: "She was an urban guerilla," adding that "it was also 'a raging against the dying of the light.'"[4]

Speakers made clear in remembering Dorothee that despite her fundamental militance, she was open to everything, was never locked in dogmatically fixed positions. Janet Walton recalled: "She had open windows, and she let the whole world come into her strong and fragile person." Strong and fragile—that is how many of her American friends remember her. Whence came this strength and this courage to expend every last bit of her energy the way she did, to take on state and civil authorities with so little protection? The solidarity of the grass-roots movements and the liberal protective embrace of Union Seminary may have contributed to it. But Janet Walton discerned Dorothee's decisive source of strength in the mystical dimensions of her theological existence. Her mysticism pervaded her theological and political thinking. She drew strength for political activities from her mystical inner being; struggle and contemplation became the decisive features of her Christian spiritual practice. Prayer and *praxis* became one.[5]

With Dorothee's attempt to reconcile theological thinking, political activity and mystical sensibility, she had scarcely been understood in Germany. At that time there was no place for anything like this in church and politics there. But at Union she regularly offered seminars on mysticism together with well-known speakers from the movements for social change. One of them is the Roman Catholic priest Daniel Berrigan, by then already one of the icons of the American protest movement.[6] With his brother Philip and other peace activists he had protested against the war in Vietnam in actions such as the burning of draft cards at Catonsville, Maryland in 1969. For many years he was incarcerated, living underground or as a fugitive. In the 1980s he was a chaplain at one of New York's palliative care clinics. Dorothee described the evening he was a guest in her course on mysticism and revolutionary change:

> One night, Daniel Berrigan came to my class on mysticism. That course gives me much joy. We try to find the connections between the different forms of mystical thinking and the social praxis of mystical thinkers. . . . I had invited [him] for the theme of 'mysticism and resistance.' He appeared almost shy, taciturn, trying hard to avoid everything cliché-like. . . . Very down to earth. "Having both feet on the ground" doesn't quite capture it. I mean the simplicity of a poet and resistance fighter who does indeed express himself in a complex way, rich in associations, at times "darkly," . . . but who prefers to speak simply, biblically, and action-oriented. . . . His topic is "the Mysticism of Poverty." He says: "The closer we are to those who wrote the Bible, the more we are in Christ."[7]

The discussion with Berrigan was heated and controversial. Contrary to many of the seminar participants critical of the church, he considered the church the only organization where free public communication is still possible, while the institutions of the state are increasingly corrupt and militarized. The decisive point of reference of such a resistance-church is the crucified Christ. "Where do public action and mysticism find each other? one student asked.—They meet in Christ. But Christ is not without context—he is on the cross."[8]

Dietrich Bonhoeffer had already urged upon the nascent Confessing Church in the context of the German church struggle in in the 1930s that the center of the church must be the crucified Christ. Bonhoeffer's 1933 Berlin University lectures on Christology had received little attention in Germany of that time.[9] But published in English as *Christ the Center* in 1966,[10] it was one of Bonhoeffer's best-known texts in America.[11] It seemed quite possible that there, in a political Christology "from below," resisting Christendom from every era would rediscover itself.

Dorothee would come across still further traces of Dietrich Bonhoeffer in New York, not least in the worship services of the black congregations in nearby Harlem. Already in 1930–1931, when the young theologian was studying at Union, still rather elitist in his attitudes, Bonhoeffer's entire sense of the church had been deeply influenced by his experience of the black churches of Harlem. The theologian Dorothee Soelle, who simply did not fit into the traditional churches in Germany, which also found her suspect, now gained a special sense of social and emotional roots in those black churches, and a feeling of belonging she had long been missing: "For a long time, I've been going back to the black church in Harlem Canaan Baptist Church. Some of these rather sentimental melodies are kept alive by the beat and the electric organ. The slow, dirge-like singing, the grief it expresses—brings forth the most powerful feelings of trust, hope, strength: 'there is power, there is power, there is power in the blood of the lamb.' I weep and ask myself why? One reason is that I cannot imagine a white German congregation expressing so much of home, of community, of feeling responsible for one other. As if we Germans were all crippled. But I'm sure there are even more reasons to weep."[12]

13

Learning to Fly

Heart Attack

Tom told me how he thought he'd die
of the pain and the anxiety
until the ambulance arrived and a large black man
said to him, "Dad, you just do
what we tell you to . . ."

And since no stranger had ever called him Father before
Tom let the young men have their way
and let the anxiety go, though not the pain
and let himself be trussed up to the chair
and waited, wondering what'd happen next
to a certain Tom X at the clinic

And I should like to sing a song
for an unknown ambulance driver
in a city that is famed for violence,
a song for a man who bestowed a name of peace
on another member of the human family

And made him a father
so that when I went to the hospital

I could see right away that Tom must have given birth to something
though to what I am not quite sure.[1]

In the fourth year of Soelle's experiment of dividing her year between New York and Hamburg, her poetry series *Fliegen lernen* (Learning to Fly) was published. Together with her 1987 *New Yorker Tagebuch* (New York Diary), neither of which had appeared in English, these poems offer the most tangible expression of her thinking, her feelings and personal experiences at that time.[2] In addition to these sources, the memories of the men and women she was close to convey a vivid image, but one that is also full of contradictions. It is an image of a woman in mid-life who wants to learn to fly, but often also feels as if she is "walking on a thousand knives."[3]

First there are the stories of a Dorothee Soelle who breaks into the friendly, liberal Union Seminary like a whirlwind. Christopher Morse, Professor of Dogmatic Theology, team-teaches courses with her on "Doctrines about God." He leaned more to the conservative side, admired the great German theologians Friedrich Schleiermacher and Karl Barth. Barth, known for appreciating the role women played in the preparatory stages of his own theological research, had already contemptuously dismissed Dorothee Soelle's independent theological work as *Frauenzimmertheologie*!,[4] commenting to his American colleagues that she was the kind of woman the "blessed apostle" Paul had forbidden to speak in the church in Corinth.[5] Now Soelle and Morse needed to become a team, and Morse was surprised by her intelligence and scholarly acumen. They argued about political and theological issues, but with respect and fairness. At Union, people eagerly followed the progress of the courses during the semester and wondered how long this arrangement could last. At the end of one course Tom Driver, alluding to the famous line of T. S. Eliot about the world ending "not with a bang but a whimper," asked: "Well, was it a bang or a whimper?" When he heard the answer: "Both," he commented dryly: "So, who's the whimper and who's the bang?"[6]

It was difficult at that time to imagine professors at a German theological faculty interacting as informally as this. Scarcely imaginable, furthermore, was the liberal attitude at Union Seminary that allowed people to take positions for which authorities in the Federal Republic of the 1970s punished faculty and students with *Berufsverbote,* the denial of government employment or termination from tenured positions. Donald Shriver, professor of theological ethics and at the time president of Union Seminary, recalls a panel discussion in which Dorothee Soelle attacked the capitalist system in extraordinarily radical terms, calling Wall Street the satanic "Beast from the Abyss," the antagonist of God referred to in the apocalyptic writings of John. And in the front row sat Union's primary financial donors, almost all of them Wall Street brokers. "Do you realize that the people from Wall Street have just approved the funds for your professorship?" Don Shriver asked. Dorothee's response in such cases was typically "I'm not interested in knowing the specifics"; she left diplomacy and the *Realpolitik* for others to take care of. Former president Shriver comments: "We need such radical people, too; a theological institution must be able to tolerate a woman prophet."[7]

The conflict that arises during a guest lecture by Fleming Rutledge, a Union alumna, is even more difficult. The traditional pietism of the Christian faith position she presents is so massive that Dorothee, incensed, interrupts,[8] calling out the word "Christofascism." The concept catches on like wildfire and becomes the fashionable word as well as a provocative irritant at Union for an entire semester. In a paper Dorothee drafts for this discussion, she clarifies what this polemical concept signifies:

> Characteristic of Christofascism is that all the roots that Christianity has in the First Testament, in the Jewish Bible, have

> been cut off. Not a word about justice, no mention of the poor, whom God comes to help, very little about guilt and suffering, no hope for the messianic realm. Hope is completely individualized, reduced to personal success. Jesus, separated from the Old Testament, becomes a sentimental figure. The senseless repetition of his name has the effect of a drug, it changes nothing and no one. . . . This kind of religion knows the cross only as a magical symbol of what He has done for us, not as a sign of the poor One who was tortured to death as a political criminal, like thousands today who stand up for his truth. . . .[9]

These statements were part of a polemic against a kind of religiosity that became the basis of a national ideology under the Ronald Reagan presidency in the 1980s. It continues today in American right-wing fundamentalism. Thus the concept of Christofascism itself became part of a political-theological debate, understandable in this context. Nevertheless, the rage of the speaker and the embarrassment of the president are also understandable. Here a guest had been insulted. Shriver pointed out to Dorothee that the issue here was not judging the merits of different positions at all, but adhering to the rules of etiquette. Dorothee was unmoved. Ethics was more important than etiquette, she replied, adding that after all, Shriver himself was responsible for theological ethics, even in this context. And a few days later, students sat in lecture halls wearing hand-printed t-shirts with the slogan: "Ethics, not Etiquette!"[10] Things heated up at Union; the revolts of the 1960s did not leave the theological seminaries unaffected. And Dorothee, well-bred daughter from a fine home, enjoyed her new-found freedom, sometimes behaving rather naughtily. "Christopher, you old fucker!" she called out across the table at a tea party with friends at the home of Paul and Marion Lehmann. For the elderly couple, who had been close friends of Dietrich Bonhoeffer in the 1930s and who now belonged to the core of the American Left, this went too far! She was never invited to their home again.

Overall, however, admiration and affection prevailed, so that Soelle was offered a full professorship with tenure at Union. For in the meantime, she was just as well known in church circles in the United States as in her own country, and just as controversial. The first American translations of her books and poems began to appear, and she was invited more and more frequently to give lectures and public readings. She traveled far and wide across the United States and Canada. Politically, she focused in these years on solidarity with the Latin American liberation movements, and in turn with the North American "Sanctuary" movement, which was supported and carried out primarily by church groups assisting political refugees to escape the war and poverty zones of Central America. "Sanctuary" congregations provided these refugees and illegal immigrants with shelter and work opportunities and protected them from the authorities' grasp. This was considered illegal by the U.S. government[11] and those involved eventually were taken to court. Dorothee reported: "Next week I'm going to Phoenix and Tucson, Arizona, to support the trial against the accused criminals. They are Christians who hide political refugees from El Salvador and Guatemala, who have no immigration papers, in churches. They are turning the churches into a sacred place (*sanctuarium)* again, where the state is not welcome."[12] The misery of refugees became a major issue for her. Again she was reflecting about the subject of "home," but also working out old guilt. In a 1985 text she wrote for the American Sanctuary Movement, Dorothee's reflection on the question of "home" becomes a prayer:

> When I was a child, Jewish people in Germany had no place to hide. If you ask me what the churches in those days did, I cannot think of anything to say. There was no refuge in that country, there was no holy place where one could hide and feel protected for a while. I am reading in "the book" that a

> people without a vision dies.[13] But a people without a sacred space, safe from murderers is already dead.
>
> God bless the Sanctuary Movement. May God make His face to shine upon all those who willingly become illegal for the sake of those the State deems illegal. May she comfort all those who have lost their homeland. God bless us all, who long for home, and lead us to a land in which there is sacred space.[14]

Tirelessly, Dorothee recalled the stories of refugees from the Bible, but she also reminded audiences of the earliest American ideals. After all, she noted, these words of Emma Lazarus are engraved on the Statue of Liberty in New York Harbor: "Give me your tired, your poor, your huddled masses yearning to be free. . . . Send these, the homeless, tempest-tossed to me."[15] At public events and press interviews surrounding the Tucson trial of the Sanctuary defendants, discussion always centered on the connections between politics, religion and the law. Dorothee was all too familiar with this debate. "Do you act from political or religious motives?" the reporters asked. The judges said, "This case is not about religion, but about violations of the law"; Dorothee did not want to allow these distinctions. But even within the Sanctuary Movement there were groups that did not want to be politically "co-opted." Dorothee wrote them a letter after her experiences in Tucson:

> I am still thinking about the tensions between the Chicago group and the Tucson group. . . . I have the impression that most people [in both groups] simply want to become disciples of Christ, men and women following Christ in a practical sense of doing mercy. . . . As I have thought about the spiritual situation of these grass-roots workers in the movement I thought of the Bible, particularly the structure of the New Testament. If you compare the first three gospels with the letters of Paul, you will find a similar tension between the Good

News, the healing, the feeding, doing the work of God on the one hand, and on the other hand the reflection and practice of the Apostle Paul. . . . I think the difference between Paul and his friends in Rome, Corinth and Chicago, on the one hand, and the friends of Jesus in Galilee and Tucson, on the other hand, is one of *theory* and *organization.* Both are necessary steps that grow out of the responsibility we have to love our neighbors as ourselves. . . . I think the early Christians had to make a conscious decision to do both—the theory and the organization of love. It was a conscious choice to engage in socio-political analysis that was already present in Christ's teaching, and also to move toward organization, which was then given the name "ecclesia," "church."[16]

The refugees were present even in Dorothee's most personal writings. She could no longer imagine a separation between faith, political engagement and private happiness. She wrote the following poem for her American friend Jim Wallace, whom she had met in 1978 at a gathering of the Religious Socialists in Washington, D.C.

I'd have liked to show you the magnolias on Broadway
and taken you to the old jeweler from 123d Street
who wants to repair my bracelet because I like him
I don't speak German
in Central Park even tulips are loveable

Everything beautiful lives fast here
maybe we don't even have time
for the short New York spring
if we listen to the refugees
who must get their stories across
and can't get over their fear

The students gave me a cross
a man wore it

who was murdered in Chile
for a while now
it's with me

I'd have liked to show you the magnolias blooming
right in the middle of the street
and would have taken you to friends
who live for a while with the refugees

I believe less and less in the kind of happiness
that two keep all to themselves
and more and more in the short shared kind
that the stories from cellars and camps fall into
and the magnolia blossoms on the street.[17]

At Dorothee's burial service twenty-five years after their first meeting, Jim would lay a magnolia blossom on her grave in memory of that short, shared happiness and in memory of their long connection based on standing up for the justice that transcends death: "I miss her greatly. But as she would recall about Joe Hill[18] in talking with me about the meaning of resurrection, she is as 'alive as you and me.'"[19]

"A theological institution must be able to tolerate a woman prophet" (Donald Shriver, former president of Union Theological Seminary, New York).

14
Between Worlds

Poet and union leader Joe Hill, executed in 1915 in a case of what has been called judicial murder, remains an icon of the American labor movement. A song dedicated to him proclaims that he will never really die: "From San Diego up to Maine, in every mine and mill, where working men defend their rights, it's there you find Joe Hill."[1] Joan Baez performed this song at the legendary 1969 Woodstock Festival, dedicating it to the young Americans who chose to go to jail rather than fight in Vietnam. At that time the Peace and Labor movements became allies for good, since it was abundantly clear that the pauperization of broad sectors of the population was the direct consequence of the arms build-up and of war. Church-based resistance circles rediscovered the biblical "shalom," the indissoluble link between justice and peace, and action groups sprang up on this foundation. Dorothee Soelle now immersed herself once again in American reality as she joined such peace and justice groups, but now in quite a different way. This process would take her into areas of personal crisis, making her travel between her rather different public and private lives.

In the late 1970s she met and came to admire Dorothy Day, the grand old lady of the Catholic Worker Movement. Day was the very embodiment of radical political engagement, mystical piety and a

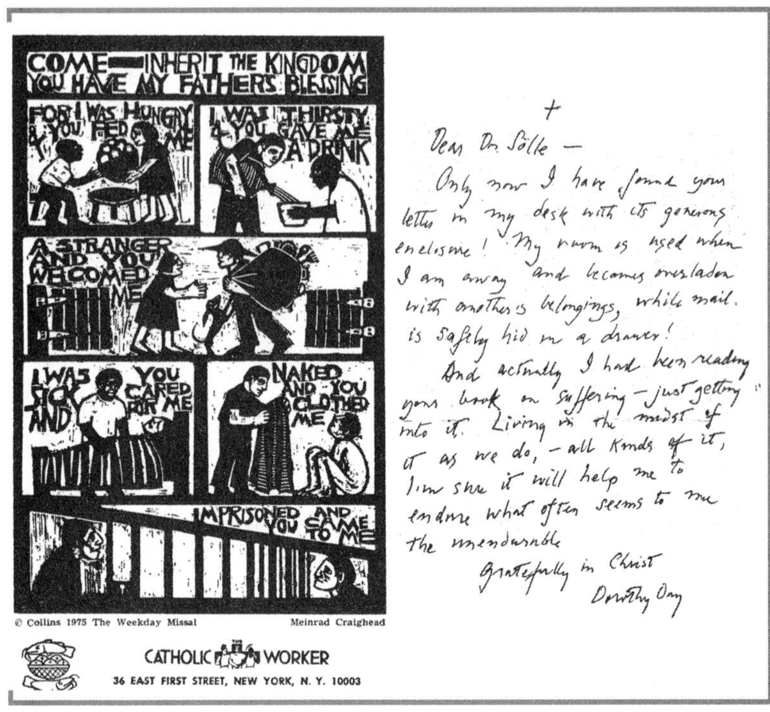

+

Dear Dr. Sölle —

Only now I have found your letter in my desk with its generous enclosure! My room is used when I am away and becomes overladen with another's belongings, while mail is safely hid in a drawer!

And actually I had been reading your book on suffering — just getting into it. Living in the midst of it as we do, — all kinds of it, I am sure it will help me to endure what often seems to me the unendurable.

Gratefully in Christ

Dorothy Day

Front and back of a postcard Dorothee Soelle received from Dorothy Day, the grand old lady of the Catholic Worker Movement. Dorothy Day's fusion of radical political engagement, mystical piety, and a lifestyle of voluntary poverty impressed Soelle very much.

life of voluntary poverty. While initially rooted in New York City's Bohemian Leftist scene, after her conversion to Roman Catholicism, Dorothy Day practiced an anarchist and pacifist Christianity that made a deep impression on Dorothee Soelle. A friend took Soelle along "into the poorest quarter in South Manhattan, to the Catholic Worker's soup kitchen":

> I served soup there along with others, mostly young volunteers. What I liked especially was that older people did not have to stand in line to be served, but were invited to

> sit at table where we served them. I carried on a long conversation with then eighty-two-year-old Dorothy Day, constantly interrupted by the people from the homeless shelter who came in and out. For the first time in my life, I came to understand what voluntary poverty means. Dorothy Day mentioned in passing that people come into her room all the time, live there for a while, take some things and leave others. The renunciation of property that she practiced included the renunciation of a private space. . . . What I also learned from this remarkable woman is that spirituality is a movement of the Spirit that does away with the separation between inward and outward life. . . . In spirituality, what is inward is to become outward, visible and audible. When we learn to share pain and joy with others, everyday life is hallowed."[2]

Yet however much Dorothee strove to adopt for herself the ideals of her great namesake, she never managed more than occasional excursions into the world of the poor, who essentially remained strangers to her. Between the Lower East Side where she volunteered in the soup kitchen, and the Theatre District where she went to hear the New York Philharmonic, was a gulf defined by more than a mere few city blocks. In Manhattan the greatest social contrasts exist in the most confined area, namely the immigrant neighborhoods, still as impoverished as ever, next to the lavish residences on the Upper East Side; Hell's Kitchen next to the financial district; luxurious Fifth Avenue parallel to the Bowery and its homeless people living in their cardboard boxes. The run-down infrastructure of public utilities like the subway, the streets, roads, bridges and electric grids stand out in contrast to the cathedrals of power and consumption. New York is known as "Babylon on the Hudson"; already in biblical times, Babylon is the stony symbol of the center of power, of a mega-culture that with its force and seductive power produces poverty and dependency in the world around it.

And just as in the days of early Christianity a culture of resistance arose against the domination of Rome's imperial culture, here, too, in this context, countercultures have always developed, borne by many people, among them actively engaged Christian women and men. Undoubtedly the most radical form of this counterculture was Dorothy Day's lifestyle in which poverty became a spiritual ideal. Dorothee Soelle did not practice this lifestyle. And when she idealizes it, her radicalism is more verbal than lived and at times even stands in contradiction to her own life.

This contradiction would not be worthy of reproach, had Dorothee not formulated her claim to this ideal in such radical terms, or if there were any evidence of her critically examining her own inconsistency. But in fact her claims and her reality clash again and again. The woman who advocates so forcefully for the poor and their cause has her difficulties with the actual manifestations of poverty: "Although I am really tired, I accompany Darleen (a nun from the Sanctuary Movement)[3] to a vesper service of the *Catholic Worker*, a simple liturgy. There's a Scripture reading, a few thin voices singing to a guitar. Those of us present include a taciturn vagrant, a neurotic forty year-old woman who absolutely wants to consume all of the communion wine, a single woman with a six year old who produces unspeakable noises through his nose. . . . A very old woman from the neighborhood joins us; Maria, one of the nuns, leads the service and plays the guitar. No one makes a fuss over the distractions; I ask myself what humility is."[4]

The subject of difficulties with humility recurs regularly in Dorothee's *New Yorker Tagebuch*. Dorothee, who wants to "learn to fly,"[5]—poetically and spiritually speaking—who also enjoys her growing fame, was sometimes in danger of taking off in rather unspiritual ways in the process. She received many invitations to speak and she, who had at first been loath to miss a single opportunity for encounter and exchange, began to show signs of elitism. On one occasion she lamented to her diary: "The organization of my visit leaves much to be desired . . . a lecture in the church filled to only one-third of its capacity. It's odd, I'm so used to crowds of people, excitement, and expectations that it's frustrating to speak only to seventy or so."[6] Even though Dorothee, the "grassroots" worker, hailed the simple life, she still thought it should look like the alternative culture she had developed for herself. And many found her rigorous critique of people who did not live up to her own lifestyle and the way she thought short on humility. The "revolutionary impatience"[7] that made her so likable sometimes turned into an intolerance that alienated even friends and sympathizers.

Then there was her zeal to convert people. Above all, it thoroughly undermined the dialogue she was beginning to have with the labor movement about its theory and praxis. While Christians in the peace and liberation movements of the 1960s and 1970s had learned to see themselves as part of larger social and political emancipation processes, Latin American liberation theology now introduced notions of a revolutionary Christian identity that clearly included missionizing features. When Arturo Maduro from Venezuela came to New York and gave a lecture about the new unity between Christians and Marxists in the Latin American liberation movements, Dorothee argued that dialogue and mutual respect were no longer the central issue for her. Her diary describes the scene: "I ask him when we should go a step further and convert the Marxists. I argue that the human being without religion (in this case I make an exception and say "the man" without religion) is, after all, rather incomplete. Great commotion among my colleagues and the students; they take me for what they used to call a *piet-cong* in Germany—a naïve, pre-scientific, Bible-believing, party-line leftist!"[8]

And in her argumentation and attitude she did indeed approach those of fundamentalism. When Fidel Castro manifested a new openness to and respect for Christianity in his "Night conversations" with the Brazilian Dominican priest Frei Betto,[9] for Dorothee this did not go far enough: "Beyond the alliance where Christians and Marxists find themselves united against the same enemies, a new identity is emerging in which people are revolutionaries in order to become Christians."[10] Jan Rehmann,[11] an early proponent of Christian-Marxist dialogue from the ranks of the "Christians for Socialism" movement, retorted that this was the same old juxtaposition of "enlightenment" and "faith," "science" and "myth" as before. "The deficits of Marxism are associated with rationalism (partiality, patriarchy, industrialism, domination of nature) and the opportunities for renewal are paired with the thread of mysticism and religion (holistic, feminine, ecological). And so the Christian solution of Marxist problems is already embedded in the diagnosis."[12] Rehmann also argued that Soelle's Christian-revolutionary idea brought together everything "that is attractive in the alternative milieu of the 'new social movements' . . . Who wants to speak up against concepts like 'holistic,' 'unifying,' 'vulnerability,' or 'experience-related'? We all want to step out into the open, for heaven's sake! And the opposite viewpoint is articulated in such a way that one can only be against it: 'rationalism,' 'faith in science,' 'patriarchal,' 'closed-minded.' Such juxtaposed binaries gloss over the conceptual difficulties of achieving a First World liberation theology for today, instead of holding them up to the light."[13]

A number of Dorothee Soelle's American friends also parted company with her on this issue. Janet Walton said that one does not have to be a Christian in order to do what is right. At this time, Beverly Harrison was living with a friend from the Communist movement and they agreed on the following mealtime prayer: "Some have bread and some have none—God bless the revolution."[14] She found Dorothee's rigorism rather out of touch with life. Indeed, the life of Dorothee Soelle the revolutionary and mystic did not measure up to steep demands. Unless one utterly withdraws from the privileges of the mainstream, compromises are unavoidable and one should admit this honestly to oneself and also to others.

Fundamentally, Dorothee knew full well the cost of being torn between mystic selflessness and elitist love of self. The entry in her New York journal on Reformation Day 1985 begins with a clear-sighted self-analysis: "Writing-crisis, Going-on-as-usual-crisis. In what direction am I being pushed?" She explores the political, aesthetic, and spiritual dimensions of the crisis and in the process also comes to face her own contradictoriness: "My lack of discipline, of spiritual order bothers me—I have no 'rule.' . . . I am not religiously strong within myself, am no guru, no 'spiritual leader' even though I am often taken for that. Helpless when invited to offer prayer at meals; at a loss, often impatient, when facing others' soul-crises. My lack of discipline within shows itself on the outside as a deep inattentiveness." She decided to use her journal-writing to learn "heavenly book-keeping," including such rules as the following: "Write every day. Endure what is gray, wretched. Don't deny the base, humiliating feelings—the reflexes of the bourgeoisie within me; acknowledge the reality of what the good old mystics called 'the stirrings of the flesh.' Love happiness (*das Glück*)! Name it! Even in small doses! There is a point I want to reach that is beyond arrogance and self-hatred."[15]

After ten years in New York, Dorothee had plumbed the possibilities and boundaries of freedom; she had experienced the multiplicity of different relationships and the loneliness of temporary singleness, hectic activity and exhaustion, revolutionary élan and its disillusionment. And, in the end, the journey between her worlds had not only been stimulating. A life divided between Hamburg and New York had brought its own stresses and strains and led to a split between her ways of life and the worlds she lived in. In the long run, you simply cannot make room for half the world in a single life's journey. Neither do two different lifestyles lived concurrently make it possible to find home and identity. There comes a time when marriage and family, too, need a shared house again, furnished and lived in together. Dorothee's decision to return for good to Hamburg was not least a conscious choice for her life together with Fulbert

Steffensky, for having a good basis for their successful life together and their shared work within the human family that had grown up around them. It seems that Dorothee needed her wild New York years in order to be able to put down roots and be at home in Hamburg for the rest of her life. In December 1985 she bade farewell to New York. Once again, she speaks in her journal about her longing for *Heimat*—home—but of course in the end not without a little bit of restiveness of heart that cannot find complete peace anywhere in the world. She spent her last evening in New York in the German House of New York University, where a memorial celebration was being held for her old friend, Nobel Prize-winning writer Heinrich Böll. The Greenwich Village subway station was closed and she had to walk through the city at night. "Walking through the night is like a farewell. . . . Good bye, Babylon on the Hudson. Good bye, my spiritual orphans, you students. Good bye, *compañeras*. Someone tonight said that literary critics had called Böll 'provincial,' but that in reality he was international. I sensed within me a little bit of envy for a sort of provincial home that I do not have. But then who really wishes such a thing as to be fully 'at home' in this world?"[16]

Songs of the wind 2

My oldest friend the riotous wind
has come again to manhattan
magnificently he whistles and whines
on my rattling window latch
and on the old air conditioner
he drums his long solo

I want to embrace you
old friend of my mother the earth
(that I have not touched for three weeks)
and spend the night with you
drunk and filled with laughter
while you crack your jokes

If in manhattan there were not
some ten thousand others
many of them confused and very old
without shelter
without protection
against your boisterous embraces

If the government had not just
forbidden these very people
to appear in a film of the UN
next to the poor of calcutta
and of west africa[17]

15

The Earth Belongs to God

The first time Dorothee Soelle and her "best friend," Luise Schottroff, appear in public together like this, sitting next to each other on the podium, is at the twenty-first Protestant *Kirchentag* in 1985 in Düsseldorf. They have known and loved each other for a long time already but now they have become inseparable as a female Bible study duo, and at every *Kirchentag* they fill huge halls. Attempts to sideline them in minor venues result in the crowds of attendees having to be redirected into the much larger halls or tents. And the beginning of their joint *Kirchentag* work is also beset with various forms of resistance, which the two encounter with feminine cunning.

Until Düsseldorf, Dorothee Soelle had never received an official invitation to appear as a presenter at any *Kirchentag* gathering. The planners of this year's event did not really want to include her this time either. So Luise Schottroff stepped in; as a professor of New Testament who had been asked to lead one of the Bible studies, she registered herself and Dorothee Soelle together as a team. No sooner had the *Kirchentag* administration swallowed this pill than they were handed a second one. The official motto of the gathering was "The Earth is the Lord's!" But the two women gave their Bible study on this topic a different title: "The Earth Belongs to God!" God is different,

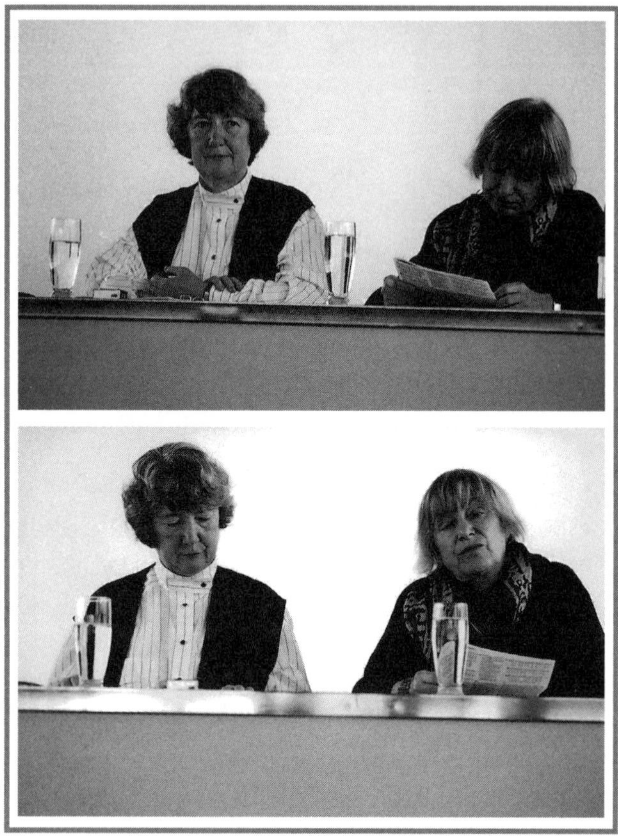

Luise Schottroff and Dorothee Soelle at one of their famous dialogical Kirchentag *Bible studies*

not merely "man" (male), and not merely "Lord." They attribute to God feminine, sisterly and brotherly qualities. Luise Schottroff began one of her Bible studies: "I want to talk of my brother God, of Jesus. I could also say 'my sister God,' for Jesus is not a god for men or for domination who makes human beings even smaller than they already are. My brother God, Jesus, has an ordinary, everyday Jewish name: Jesus, Jeshua, 'God helps.'"[1]

Dorothee Soelle explained why she preferred not to use the title "Lord" in connection with God: "There is a male theology that thinks of God primarily as one giving commands and orders, as an omnipotent power, an imperial ruler. I want to call this theology 'God-imperialism,' because I believe that it functions ideologically exactly like imperialism does in the world of business and politics, namely to subjugate human beings. . . . To believe in God in terms of this imperialist theology means to subject oneself to things as they are, just as one subjects oneself to bad weather, to paying taxes and to technological constraints. This kind of piety says: There must be some purpose in this; there's no other way to understand it. That is why fatalism is the flip side of God-imperialism."[2]

Thus the reformulation of the concept of God and of God-language was not only a feminist agenda. Soelle was not really a feminist, nor is Schottroff. They are much more part of the bedrock of a generation of women who in their time set out on a new path of freedom from oppression in general. They were among the few women who emancipated themselves in both the academic and the social sphere, opening up new territories that had essentially been open only to men. At the same time, they were active in political resistance movements and took positions that made them suspect to the established powers and institutions. They learned over and over again through everyday experience that the repression and intrigues that came their way were at the same time expressions of men's power and men's fear, and that the abuse of power and arbitrary actions in university, church, and politics were also manifestations of sexism.

Accordingly, feminism was part of a necessary movement of liberation, but they felt it must not be restricted to the liberation of women alone. In a letter to the New York Women's Center, Dorothee Soelle had already distanced herself from any feminism that concerned itself exclusively with the rights and needs of women. She was once invited to speak about the women of Nicaragua at an event sponsored by the Women's Center. When she learned that men were not allowed into the building, she wrote: "This is not my feminism! I understand that we need a certain limited time apart. It has to do with how we want to define who we ourselves are as women, with the search for our identities. But when separation becomes separatism, when it is the rule rather than the exception, something of the integrity of our struggle is lost. Feminism then becomes a biological category, another breed of racism. . . . For me feminism is a human enterprise. . . . God needs all her children so that they can become free from fear and hatred, so that we may finally grow together into a space free from domination."[3]

To be able to conceive of God in feminine terms would have been unthinkable for Dorothee before her encounters and experiences in the American women's scene. Beverly Harrison in particular asked her again and again: What does your theology have to do with your being a woman? This is yet another aspect of Dorothee's development, quite different from the struggle against sexist marginalization in church and university. It was no longer a matter of being acknowledged for having proven oneself able "to be a real man" in the world of men. What counted now was realizing one's own feminine abilities, realizing gender difference with the goal of using these productively, both in togetherness and in opposition to one another. Beverly preached that women ought no longer let themselves be trivialized and robbed of their importance.

Dorothee's insight during her New York years into women's significance in their own right, with or without a male partner, was not only a way of thinking for her, it was a new life experience. There she found an evolving women's world that did not hate men, but that was able to get along quite well without them. For Dorothee, who had hitherto existed primarily as a wife and mother and who experienced the absence of a man or husband more as a deficit, these were new and inspiring worlds. Women sat together in a bar, took trips and went to the movies, planned projects and publications, and were relaxed hosts in their own cluttered flats. One of Dorothee's favorite American expressions at this time was, "a woman without a man is like a fish without a bicycle!" Another was, "when God made man, she was only practicing."[4] Women's worship services with their own topics and rituals emphasized the significance of women's particular experience: pregnancy and birthing, abortion and sexual assault. The discovery of feminine spirituality went hand in hand with the insight that God is much more than a man. Thinking of God in female terms and concepts, rediscovering the feminine sides of God that are already represented in biblical traditions, uncovering the dimensions of women's lives hidden away in biblical texts, and digging up the buried story of women in the history made and written by men—all this now became the theme of a feminist theology determined to remain faithful to the biblical traditions instead of replacing them with goddess mythology and witches' magic.

In the introduction to their first book of Bible studies, *Die Erde gehört Gott: Texte zur Bibelarbeit von Frauen* (The Earth Belongs to God: Texts to Accompany Bible Study by Women), Dorothee Soelle and Luise Schottroff stated clearly that the feminist perspective must be a component of any comprehensive liberation theology approach.

> The basis of our Bible studies is a liberation-theological hermeneutic, that is, a historical and theological method that goes together with the theology of liberation and feminist theology. The Bible holds a significant position in the movements of liberation. One aspect of liberation-theological hermeneutic is to take the situations of the people who appear in the Bible and their time just as seriously as those of today's people who learn from the Bible what it means that faith in God and Christ can move mountains. Thus, this hermeneutic proceeds using social historical methods in order to give ourselves and others an account of our own society's situation. . . . Biblical texts are testimonies, the witness of people directly affected, telling the unvarnished truth about their

> own situation. They clearly express what faith and hope in God mean in practical terms and what liberating steps are connected with that faith and hope in everyday life. Therefore, interpreting the Bible must remain accountable to two different contexts: one's own, and that of the people whose voices are heard in the Bible. For both of them faith cannot be divorced from everyday reality, the real situation of people that is determined by brutal violence, in most cases through economic, political and military means. God's word burst in then and bursts in now upon this situation. . . . Wherever one speaks of faith, the respective political and social conditions must be named for what they are.[5]

This, then, is the consciousness with which Dorothee Soelle traveled back and forth between New York and Hamburg in the late 1970s and 1980s when so much was happening politically and socially on both continents. What do the political and social conditions in Germany look like at this time? Since the beginning of the 1980s, hundreds of thousands had taken to the streets in the Federal Republic, driven by concern for peace and security in Europe. For the first time, people and groups who had previously distanced themselves from or even fought against one another now joined forces. Leftists of all shades became allies: Christians and Socialists, peace and solidarity movements, the ecological and women's groups were in league together. The immediate reason for this was the "twin-track' decision of NATO on December 12, 1979, that envisioned, among other things, stationing in West Germany a new generation of mid-range nuclear ballistic missiles intended to assure the United States the option of a first strike against the Soviet Union should the two superpowers exchange fire with atomic weapons. Thus the missiles' purpose was to make a nuclear war possible. The decision to station the cruise and Pershing missiles in West Germany not only provoked a new round of the arms race, but, what is more, American military strategists consciously put the existence of Europe at risk, defining it as a nuclear battlefield. Secret Pentagon papers lay out quite openly the aims of a "first-strike" strategy. The targeted nuclear strike against what President Reagan called the "evil empire," the apocalyptic "battle of Armageddon" proclaimed by the fundamentalist U.S. President, was elevated to the realm of possibility. At the same time, the missiles policy accelerated the production of arms in order to bring the Soviet Union to its knees for good economically by forcing it to "arm itself to death." A further step of this escalation, "Star Wars," was included in American strategic planning. Many Germans opposed to the arms race found their mood at the beginning of the 1980s captured well in the last poem penned by the then terminally ill Berlin poet Volker von Törne:

> What then, old Törne, keeps you yet from death?
> The terror struts about with newest weapons
> Raw fear is borne on wings and rage is cold . . .[6]

Dorothee Soelle was among those who embodied the voice of hope and resistance in this time of fear and cold rage. Joining other well-known women and men in politics, church, science and the arts, she participated in blockade actions by the anti-nuclear movement of American military bases in Germany. With her friend Heinrich Böll and other prominent Germans—Walter Jens,[7] Peter Härtling,[8] Heinrich Albertz[9] and Erhard Eppler[10]—she sat at the entrance to the Mutlangen air base near Stuttgart on September 1, 1983, where the new Pershing II missiles were to be stationed. All blockaders were "hauled off," arrested and tried in court. In November 1985, Dorothee was sentenced in absentia for "Nötigung"—compulsion with reprehensible intent—and was charged a fine of 2000 German Marks (about $2800 at that time) for the police detachments sent to control the protesters for ten days. The news of the fine reached her in New York during her final term there. Spontaneously, Don Shriver offered to help: "If you have to pay this, please, remember that you have good friends here."[11] That same evening, she gave an address entitled "Ein Volk ohne Vision geht zugrunde" (A People without a Vision Comes to Ruin). Dorothee's call for prophetic speaking truth to power, taken from Proverbs 29:18 ("Where there is no prophecy, the people cast off restraint, but happy are those who keep the law" [of righteousness]),[12] recurred in many of her subsequent speeches in the West German peace movement. There she called not only for the end of what she called a kind of "suicidal tolerance of the murder industry and those who run it," for resistance against the military-industrial complex, but also for a reorientation of politics and the economy on a global scale: "What would it look like, this land, in which it would be easier to be good? . . . The land where it would be easier to be good would uncompromisingly take the side of the poor in the negotiations for a new economic world order, instead of securing the developing nations as markets for its own and for transnational companies and then selling this plot to us as 'security policy.'[13]

The arms-race madness militarizes brains, endangers peace, produces poverty and hunger, and smothers humans and nature with death, argued Soelle. "The arms race kills even without war"—which became the title of a 1982 book.[14] "The bombs are falling *now*!" More and more, the understanding of these global connections enters into the churches' discussions as well. At the 1983 Hannover *Kirchentag,* the "triumphal march" of the "lila Tücher" (purple scarves) through the churches began; written in large letters on the scarves worn or waved by participants was the clear demand to reject new weapons of mass destruction on European soil: "ein *Nein* ohne jedes Ja zu neuen Massenvernichtungswaffen!" (a clear no—without any kind of yes to new weapons of mass destruction!). The distinguished physicist and philosopher-statesman Carl Friedrich von Weizsäcker[15] then addressed the 1985 Düsseldorf *Kirchentag,* taking up one of Dietrich Bonhoeffer's ideas from the early 1930s. Bonhoeffer had tried already at that time to rally the churches of the *oikumene*. When wars threaten and human rights are manifestly violated, Bonhoeffer argued, an ecumenical council of churches must resort to direct political action; it must make engagement for peace and human rights a necessary element of confessing faith in Christ. Weizsäcker's address some five decades later gave further public impetus to what soon became known as the Conciliar Process for Justice, Peace, and the Integrity of Creation (JPIC).[16] What had been a process among individuals and groups in the Protestant churches in both German states subsequently grew into a broad-based grassroots movement in both the Protestant and Roman Catholic churches. Politically conservative groups looked on it with suspicion and in some instances openly attacked it; they sought instead to explain the state of the world in terms of humanity having fallen into sin. Dorothee Soelle offers a rebuttal to the proponents of this view:

> God who makes a new beginning in spite of sin is not being taken seriously at all, even though his name occurs now and then. For in this view God has already been turned into fate. This theology is a theology of death; it does not ally us with God for the sake of life. . . . This theology's most important subject is subjective sin and the objective powerlessness of human beings. Its most important praxis is the accommodation to sin, whether with or without weapons, with or without arms exports, with or without profiting from the arms trade. But the God of the Bible is the power of life that transforms our hearts . . . This God does not show up at all in the theology of death. Of course sin rules over us in a society that systematically educates human beings to lie and, aided by the media, to deny reality, a society that systematically turns the relationships of love into consumer goods for sale and portrays murder on command—the nuclear first strike—as our defense. The question is only whether this talk of sin is godless, without liberation, as it is in the accommodated churches, or whether it is rooted in God's covenant with us—that is, in liberation.[17]

A Prayer Based on the Ninetieth Psalm

Lord, you have been our dwelling place in all generations
before the mountains were brought forth and the oceans
before our little blue planet
on which life multiplies through love and union
was born from you after a long pregnancy
you were there waiting for us
you allow people to die and call others into being
come again, you children of adam and eve
you allow cultures to perish
when they separate from you
and you call others into being
What seems to us a thousand years and unchanging
bloody violence
is to you a short watch in the night[18]
even tyrants break down exhausted
business conglomerates dissolve

and the knowledge of infallible parties
becomes last year's snow
slavery was profitable and flourished
but in the evening of your day it had withered
the fruits of armaments climbed to the sky
but your rage consumes them
and your wrath will destroy their stolen prosperity
you make known our plundering of the poor
you bring to light our well veiled crimes
so our time flies fast in fear of the truth
we spend our years as if on a drug trip
that tips into terror[19]

16

The God of Liberation

As a result of encountering liberation theology, Dorothee Soelle's political theology had changed in several respects by the 1980s. While at first it had been predominantly influenced by systematic reflections on a new Christology, now a "relecture," a rereading of Scripture against the background of a liberation theological praxis, gradually brought the Bible as a whole back into view. And while her theological approach to "vicarious representation" had radically relativized the significance of God in favor of a "christological reduction," now faith in the God of Israel found a new voice and, with it, the liberating traditions of both testaments. Finally, Luise Schottroff's social-historical and feminist exegesis led Dorothee to trace the buried history of women and opened her eyes for "the God of the people at the bottom."

Against that liberation theological background, Dorothee Soelle once again looked at the sufferings and struggles, the defeats and the liberation experiences of the people of Latin America's base communities, but now in a new way. In the context of the suffering and dying people she saw there, the question arose for her what resurrection might mean. In her poem "Arguments for Overcoming Powerlessness" she formulated some thoughts about this, though still very cautiously:

Arguments for Overcoming Powerlessness

We can hold out longer
we need a better future
among us are the people with worse wounds
the victims of capitalism
among us someone once
passed out bread enough for everyone

We can hold out longer
we are building the human city
with us are allies of the disenfranchised behind walls

and those in the cities driven from their lands
to us belong the dead of the second world war
who want something to eat at last and justice
among us someone rose once
from the dead[1]

In this context the political theology of the 1968 generation flowed into the broad stream of the newly emerging liberation-theological spirituality. There was no longer any dualism of "this-worldly" and "other-worldly" about resurrection hope. Being resurrected into life became the central experience of faith, but not merely as an individual experience. Now it also meant overcoming death-dealing economic and social structures. Correspondingly, sin was more than an individual person's failing; it was also and above all recognized as a structural problem: "We do not understand sin as a matter of individual issues, nor as that global Protestant feeling of powerlessness that says that after all, our human strength cannot accomplish anything. . . . We are collaborators in sin simply by belonging to the rich Northern world."[2]

In the summer of 1983 Dorothee Soelle was invited by the World Council of Churches (WCC) to address its Sixth General Assembly in Vancouver, British Columbia (Canada). In a July 27 plenary session,

"We are collaborators in sin simply by belonging to the rich Northern world." With such statements Dorothee Soelle provoked the conservative forces in church and society of the Federal Republic.

she delivered an address entitled "Life in its Fullness," which soon appeared in the German newspaper *Die Zeit* with the title "Wege zum Leben in seiner Fülle—Ein zorniges Plädoyer gegen Geld und Gewalt" (Paths to life in its fullness—An Outraged Plea against Money and Violence). This address once again fanned the controversy surrounding Soelle in Germany; her opening sentences alone brought the conservative powers in church and society to a white heat:

Dear sisters and brothers, I speak to you as a woman from one of the richest countries of the earth, a country with a bloody history that reeks of gas, a history that some of us Germans have not been able to forget; I come from a country that holds the greatest concentration of atomic weapons in the world, ready for use. I want to tell you something about the fears that rule in my affluent and militaristic land. I speak too out of anger, in criticism and in mourning. This pain about my country, this resistance I feel against my own society, do not arise from an arbitrary mood or because I have nothing better to do. Rather, they come from faith in the life of the world that I have encountered in the poor man from Nazareth who possessed neither wealth nor weapons. That poor man places the life of the world right before our eyes and points us to the ground of being, to God . . .

Christ came into the world so that all human beings might have life and have it in fullness (John 10:10). . . . For roughly two thirds of the human family there is no "life in its fullness" because they live in poverty, in naked economically fostered pauperization at the edge of death. They are hungry, without shelter, with no schools and no medicines for their children, no clean water to drink, no work—and they don't know how to get rid of their oppressors. Trade agreements and international relationships are imposed by the First World on the poor who sink into misery that grows worse daily. The very struggle to survive destroys fulfilled life and the Shalom of God the Bible proclaims . . .

Christ came into the world so that "all have life in fullness" but the absolute pauperization, which in our technologically developed world is a crime, destroys people's body, mind, soul, and spirit because it poisons hope and turns faith into a grotesque figure, into an impotent apathy. Between the impoverished and Christ, who signifies the fullness of life for all, exploitation intervenes as the sin of the rich as they try to destroy the promise of abundance for all.[3]

The response to this speech was vehement but also divided. Dorothee Soelle had expressed out loud what many ecumenically and politically oriented Christians in the peace and solidarity movements were thinking. Church governing bodies, however, soon distanced themselves from her, pointing out that she spoke in Vancouver as a guest of the World Council of Churches, not as a representative of the Evangelische Kirche Deutschlands (EKD), the major Protestant church structure in Germany. The Second German Television Network (ZDF)—and the BBC—the British Broadcasting Corporation—canceled programs about her and the Protestant Institute for Youth and Social Work dropped a course she was involved in so as not to endanger their relationships with the EKD. On November 3, 1983, the Protestant Press Service reported that four pastors in the Flensburg area near the Danish border "have launched a nationwide signature-campaign demanding that the EKD state publicly that the views of theologian Dorothee Soelle and 'her influential following' do not correspond to the church's basic faith statements."[4] This action was soon met with a counteraction by EKD critics which presented a challenge to the church in Germany. Now the church needed to take a clear public position. For by now, the mood and the power relationships, at least in the Protestant churches, had evolved. Clergy entering the ministry since the late 1960s were staking out new theological priorities. Some theologians—both male and female—by now even held church administrative positions or academic chairs. They were now taking positions in support of the woman who many of them had seen as the path-breaking leader and thinker in the battle for women's and human rights in both church and society.

Meanwhile a different discussion was taking place in the Roman Catholic Church. Having brought new movement into

Catholic Christianity worldwide, liberation theology was now felt by the top of the hierarchy in Rome to be a danger to the faith and the church. Pope John Paul II, who had brought to his papacy a distinct openness to the world, was nonetheless a conservative hardliner in theological and political matters. In the 1980s he turned unambiguously against the positions espoused by liberation theology. He expressed the basis for his opposition in a theological expert opinion paper issued by the Congregation for the Doctrine of the Faith, headed by Cardinal Ratzinger, later Pope Benedict XVI. In the wake of this, Brazilian theologian Leonardo Boff was forbidden to speak or publish; bishops who had still advocated for the "preferential option for the poor" at the Latin American bishops' meetings at Medellín (1968) and Puebla (1979) and had thus upheld the influence of the Catholic Church on the restless Latin American continent, were replaced upon their retirement by adherents of the conservative "Opus Dei" group.[5] Nicaragua's Catholics in particular were especially impacted by the Pope's moves; many Christians there had also participated in the Sandinista revolution and the overthrow of the Unites States–supported Somoza dictatorship in 1979, among them the priest and poet Ernesto Cardenal. He became Minister of Culture in the Sandinista government, and was therefore defrocked and removed from the priesthood. This action was part of the "crusade against Communism," a cause that Rome had taken up again with the arrival of John Paul II. There was no understanding for the urgent and fervent plea made earlier in Rome by Bishop Oscar Arnulfo Romero of El Salvador that "Latin America is not Poland." John Paul II had made no response at that time; instead he had withdrawn the protection of the church from the congregations in El Salvador, thus leaving Bishop Romero unprotected as well. Soon after, on March 24, 1980, while presiding at mass, Bishop Oscar Romero was shot to death by paramilitary forces. Now, the verdict of Rome against liberation theology and liberation movements also put the Sandinista Revolutionary government at greater risk, while initially it had been able to count on the broad affirmation of the populace. Financed and armed by the United States, the "Contras" infiltrated the country, invaded villages and parishes in nightly attacks, and murdered harvest workers and teachers in the literacy program implemented by the Sandinista government. Once again, a wave of solidarity flooded not only over Europe but also throughout the United States. Volunteers from organizations such as "Witness for Peace" were sent to Nicaragua and, in "brigades of solidarity," joined peasants in harvest labor and, even more important, by their very presence as international observers helped protect people against attacks by paramilitary groups or a direct North American invasion. And Dorothee composed her "Prayer for Nicaragua":

Prayer for Nicaragua

Spread a large blanket
over the little country of volcanoes
so that the bombers cannot find it
and the arson-murderers cannot enter
and the president of the united dead
will forget the little country

Spread a large blanket
over the little country just four years old
so that the children can attend school
and also the older women like me
so that coffee gets harvested and medicine handed out
and no one is forgotten

Spread a large blanket
held by all who love this country
the Virgin Mary has a coat
and Saint Francis a festive garment
that he threw at his rich father's feet

and Ho Chi Minh wore a peasant's shirt like Sandino
the blanket is woven of all this fabric

Spread a large blanket
of wishes breathing so much affection
that they become prayers
and love is the verb
that belongs to God
so the blanket comes from God

A dark blanket
spread to protect the hope of the poor
until the night ends
until finally the night ends[6]

17

Mysticism and Resistance

Dorothee's poem "Prayer for Nicaragua" (see p. 145), leading up to its hopeful closing line, "until finally the night ends," points to the gently sprouting seeds of hope in the late 1970s and early 1980s. The reasons for this new hope were the liberation movements that were continuing to gain strength, and the reform efforts in the Soviet Union. By breaching Cold War logic and creating a free, democratic and open Socialism, people hoped, the East-West conflict would be eliminated and there would no longer be a legitimate reason for the use of violence in the conflict between North and South. The last large-scale actions of the peace movement in West Germany were inspired by this hope. The World Council of Churches' "Conciliar Process for Justice, Peace, and the Integrity of Creation" helped unify the Christian peace groups in West and East Germany; they moved closer together in the 1980s, strengthened by the vision of Soviet President Mikhail Gorbachev, who talked of a "common house of Europe," of the need to proceed together against poverty and violence before these scourges found a new dimension in global terrorism. His words kindled optimism and enthusiasm in both East and West, but in the end, he remained a voice crying in the wilderness, ignored by history.

Ultimately it was the liberation and reform movements that foundered in face of the greater power of their opponents and, to be sure, also because of their own weaknesses and mistakes. Nicaragua, the great hope project, was the first to suffer defeat. In the late 1986 elections there the conservative forces, massively supported by the U.S. government, pushed themselves through to a narrow victory. Election observers had come from many countries to monitor the election process, among them Dorothee Soelle. She ran into Anne Barstow, wife of her New York colleague Tom Driver, who reported: "People were exhausted from the Contra War and from the consequences of the destabilization of the country."[1] When the election results were announced, Anne and Dorothee held each other and wept. It was like a harbinger of the East German *Wende*—the "turnaround" of 1989 that finally brought about the end of an era that had been marked just as much by revolutionary hopes as by disappointments, by victories as well as defeats.[2] Many people in the Western world and even more in the Third World certainly had not considered the Socialist community of states a "paradise," but nonetheless one alternative to corporatist capitalism. While in need of critique from a position of solidarity, the socialist states had every reason to claim support for their attempt to abandon the exploitative structures of the market and the banks. This was also the position of the Federation of Protestant Churches of the German Democratic Republic, believing God had called them to cooperate with the secular state in the effort, as critical GDR theologian Heino Falcke put it in a 1972 challenge to the churches, to create a "socialism capable of improvement"[3] (*verbesserlichen Sozialismus*). The catastrophes and perversions of Stalinism and those of the Maoist Cultural Revolution had long been overcome and a new generation had gathered to articulate a "new way of thinking," discussing possibilities for a Socialist politics of reform and détente. But it was too late to prevent the economic and political collapse of their society.

Dorothee's book Mystik und Widerstand, *published in 1999 (Eng.* The Silent Cry: Mysticism and Resistance*), includes her commentary on the collapse of the East German regime and the ensuing political and economic transformation known as the "Wende" that resulted in German unification in October 1990.*

In the last book published during her lifetime, *The Silent Cry: Mysticism and Resistance,* Dorothee Soelle wrote: "Since 1989, we have lived in a standardized, globalized order of technocracy that demands and achieves disposition over space, time, and creation. Its engine runs on, driven by coercion to produce more and programmed for ever more speed, productivity, consumption, and profit for about twenty percent of humankind. In all of history, this program is more efficient and more brutal than comparable engines and their towers of Babel."[4]

In the meantime, the system of globalized capitalism paraded itself in its efficiency and violence. The gap between rich and poor grew ever wider, not only between the rich countries and the regions of poverty, but also within the societies of the rich countries themselves. The marginalization of entire groups of countries and populations that were regarded as "superfluous" proceeded unabated. At the same time, waves of refugees and hunger-driven revolts, local violent conflicts and terrorism made it obvious that there would be no end to violence without first establishing justice. Faced with this reality, the search was on, not only for different forms of resistance but also for new sources of strength and motivation. Heinz Kahlau, a professed atheist and Communist, a lyric poet and pupil of Bertolt Brecht, wrote the following hopeful lines during the years of gradual stagnation and decline of the East German Democratic Republic:

Woe
when experiences
are victorious over hopes
Without hopes
no more experiences
And
where experiences end
faith begins
But that is just the place
where the future
also begins.[5]

A faith such as this had become a vital necessity, but was no longer bound to institutional faith communities. Such faith lived in the hope that the imperial powers and their towers of Babel would collapse and—like the biblical tower of Babel—would be reduced to ruins. Such faith also nourished the hope that the sighs and cries of the slaves in Egypt who had been beaten down while building the pyramids, and those of the inmates in the quarries of Flossenbürg, Mauthausen, and many other concentration camps, would reach heaven and move God to intervene, as in the often recalled biblical Exodus story of the Hebrew foreign workers' liberation from slavery.

To keep on living and acting in that faith meant persisting in the dream. One had to keep on proclaiming what utopia and vision, searching for home, yearning for peace, hungering for justice and desiring healing meant in today's world. The aim was to sow doubt about this world being the best world there is, or even the only one realistically possible. That is where, for Soelle, the journey of mysticism and resistance set out from, the "*No* to the world as it is now!"

In these years Dorothee Soelle wrote and spoke tirelessly on behalf of this resistance and this hope, and against cynicism and resignation. In an era when many resigned themselves to a life style with the economic and social privileges of the "fittest," she reminded her listeners that a people without a vision for justice and solidarity comes to ruin. This biblical theme now also remained her watchword in her uncompromising search for ways of liberation for the entire human family. This theme went hand in hand with the prophetic promise that searching continuously and passionately for God is part of this journey of liberation that one day will reach its destination: "If with all your heart you truly seek me I will surely let you find me" (Jer. 29:13-14). In this connection, Soelle now also reflected again about life's meaning in a new way, about Christ and the "far away nearby" God.

> Suffering does not necessarily separate us from God. On the contrary, it may actually put us in touch with the mystery of reality. To follow Christ means to take part in his suffering . . . *Compassio* in this sense . . . arises in the immediacy of the innocent suffering of others and from solidarity with them. . . . Without *compassio,* there is no resurrection. . . . It is not a dolorousness that seeks suffering and then chooses which one to shoulder; rather, it is a mystical approach to reality which moves one from the passive experience of being overwhelmed to a voluntary acceptance of participation in the suffering of the humiliated and insulted. . . . Acceptance deprives icy meaninglessness

In a time when many resigned themselves to live with the right of the "fittest" in the economy and in society, Soelle reminded her listeners that a people without a vision for justice and solidarity comes to ruin.

of its power, because it clings to God's warmth "even in suffering."[6] In this context "sacrifice" does not mean that . . . a saving quality accrues to suffering as such. Rather, that concept expresses the participation of humans who do not resign themselves but, in mystical defiance, compassionately insist through their suffering that nothing become lost.[7]

Here it finally became clear what ultimately had been Dorothee Soelle's most significant source of strength and inspiration all along. For one, it was the "in spite of everything" of Jewish faith that grounded the tradition of resistance of both Testaments, this "nevertheless I cleave continually to you"[8] of the human being who with stubborn tenderness cleaves even to the hidden God. Dorothee had rediscovered the liberating God of Israel in the Christian-Jewish dialogue that was existentially indispensable for her, and in her struggle to find ways of speaking about God "after Auschwitz." In the same way, she had discovered Jesus the "Jewish proletarian" who, as messianic prophet and teacher of justice, became a victim of the Roman *imperium*—and of *every* other imperial society ever since. Related to the rediscovery of Jesus as messianic Jew was her finding and valuing in a new way the gift of God's instructions, the Torah, which in its written form, the Torah scroll, was carried by the Jewish community into the Diaspora and Exile, rescued from the flames of the Warsaw Ghetto, to be brought then into a promised land. This tradition is the distinctive gift Christians and Jews can bring to humanity's dream of a new tomorrow. The other tradition is that of mysticism and resistance. Here Dorothee Soelle's visions join with those of countless other seekers of God, of truth, and of home in many countries and cultures. In trying to describe mystical experience in today's world, Dorothee finally resorted to the experience reported by a woman student in one of her American seminars:

> One winter's night, she woke up at four in the morning, went outside, and looked at the stars in the clear, frosty sky. She had a once-in-a-lifetime feeling of happiness, of being connected with all of life, with God; a feeling of overwhelming clarity, of being sheltered and carried. She saw the stars as if she had never seen them before. She described the experience in these words: 'Nothing can happen, I am indestructible, I am one with everything.' This did not happen again until . . . when,

in a different context, something similar took place. The new context was a huge demonstration against the Vietnam War. There, too, she knew that she was sheltered, as part of the whole, 'indestructible,' together with the others. Supposing this young woman had lived in fourteenth-century Flanders; she would have had other traditions of language at her disposal that would have allowed her to say: "I heard a voice" or "I saw a light brighter than everything else."[9]

Against Death

I must die
but i'm telling you
that's all
i'll do for death

I'll refuse
all other thoughts
of respecting its officials
of celebrating
its banks as people-friendly
its inventions as scientific progress

I'll resist
all the other seductions
  to mild depression
to well-oiled autonomy
to the sure knowledge
that death will win out anyway

I must die
but i'm telling you
that's all
i'll do for death

I'll laugh at it
tell stories
about how people outwitted it
and how the women
drove it away

I'll sing
and regain lost land
from death
with every note

But i'm telling you
that's all[10]

18

Dying for Light

Dorothee Soelle, Mystic and Rebel to the End

Dorothee Soelle had described the beginning of her conscious life as "darkness without beginning." At the end, she is "dying for light."

In the summer of 1993, she became gravely ill; for days she lay unconscious. After this, the themes that emerged in her life were those of "becoming lighter" and "accepting slowness." This more than anything else was infinitely difficult for her: "At the moment, growing old means for me that I grow more impatient with myself."[1] Sitting down and taking it easy was not her thing; scarcely had she recuperated a bit and she was off to present Bible studies, readings and lectures. She began to involve the "Grupo Sal" in her appearances, a group of German and Latin American musicians who has also accompanied Ernesto Cardenal on his visits to Germany for concert-readings. Two important projects came into being in these years: her autobiographical memoir: *Gegenwind: Erinnerungen,* in translation: *Against the Wind: Memoir of a Radical Christian,* and the book *Mystik und Widerstand. Du stilles Geschrei,* in translation: *The Silent Cry: Mysticism and Resistance.* Her relationship with her children was also renewed and deepened during her final years. One of her books, a travel memoir from the various countries she had visited in Latin America, begins with a poetic dedication to her daughter Caroline, who is probably most like Dorothee herself:

For Caroline in Carabuco
who does many things
that I could only dream of
and lives a few things
that I run after draped in words
suffers some things
I would like to have protected her from
gone far away and yet closer
to the memory of the fire
that we all need for life
daughters and mothers[2]

Caroline, her husband (Manuel Hilari), and their children (Miguel, Johanna and Samuel), live in the Bolivian Andes where Caroline works as a medical doctor. The honoraria and book royalties Dorothee and Fulbert received were designated for Caroline's medical project *Andean Rural Health Care.* Dorothee dedicated her memoir *Against the Wind* to her son:

Dedicated to my son Martin
the "existentialist"—
that's what a Jewish friend called him as a baby
on account of Martin Heidegger.
In the footsteps of Saint Martin of Tours,
he preferred caring for the aged
to preparing for war.
To the skeptic
who keeps his distance from his third namesake
the great Martin Luther
but not without raising protest
more politely than his mother
more restrained than his sisters
and to this very day more reliably
than all of us."[3]

However different the paths taken by each of Dorothee's children, each in their own way has taken up their mother's program of opposition to the life style of the upper middle class. Dorothee kept in regular and close touch with her other two children as well, calling them on the phone every Sunday. "She held the family together," says her daughter Mirjam Steffensky. Living close by, Mirjam, a young research scientist, and the mother of "Lottchen," had the easiest access to her mother. Dorothee was a most enthusiastic "Mumama" to her granddaughter. In Mirjam's memory, Dorothee blossomed again in all her beautiful contradictions. On the one hand she was simple and had few wants, but then would be demanding and a bit elitist. She would go out wearing something she picked up for almost nothing at a flea market, and then parade around in an expensive fur coat from a Swiss boutique. She could be both brusque and empathetic, hard as steel and vulnerable; she could be free and self-sufficient but then need protection and people she could turn to for support. In the final years of her life, one more aspect of her contradictory nature appeared: Dorothee was always searching for home, *Heimat*, and yet she ventured across numerous borders. She said once herself that having no home leads one to practice the art of boundary crossing. And in the end, the themes of her life were *Entgrenzung*—removing boundaries—and *Einwurzelung*—putting down roots; the paradox of finitude and being without boundaries.

Many external things had been clarified for her. The house in Hamburg had become a place to be "at home." She had survived the earlier controversies, or at least they had become less acerbic. Being attacked and marginalized was for the most part now a matter of history. The much maligned Dorothee Soelle had gradually become an icon honored in many contexts, "the Dorothee who belonged to all of us," as Mirjam put it with a touch of sarcasm. The "baskets full of hate letters" belonged to the past. She kept a small selection in an envelope marked "filth and rubbish." Life had become simpler in many respects; it was simply a joy to be alive at all. What does it take to be at home on earth? Some things came back to her from the first chapter of her life story: nature, flowers and grasses that luxuriate undisturbed in the garden, among them her beloved roses, *sunder warumbe*—Meister Eckhart's "without a why or wherefore," and the trees, the water, the changing light. Singing and swimming remained her passions to the very end, playing the piano, her Hamburg congregation's madrigal choir.

And, last but not least, of course, "Steff." They lived together, sometimes more, sometimes less; they laughed and cried, worked and argued together. They looked after each other, sometimes one more for the other and vice versa. All this and much more, always striving together for the vision that brought them together in the first place: "Love cannot be separated from justice, nor sexual relations from the political clarity with which we ought to live in our world. Love is no land of lotus flowers, no hiding place, no island for twosomes. Real love relates to the world. I remember a sentence from the 1968 generation: 'The more I make love, the more I want

In their last years together, Dorothee Soelle and Fulbert Steffensky appeared more and more often as a couple in dialogue sermons and conversational debates.

to make the revolution.' The more I love, the more I want another world than the one we live in. We need this undivided love for life each and every day."[4]

These words were spoken by an old woman in a sermon in Bethel, Germany, where Dorothee's disabled daughter Michaela still lives in a therapeutic residential community. The idea that each and every day of our lives we need this undivided love for life, the love that sets out to meet death head-on, stayed with Dorothee and Fulbert in their last years together. The two old lovers were now seen more and more frequently in joint presentations, well-managed conversational debates and dialogue sermons. They each had their own studies and desks, but sometimes Dorothee walked into Fulbert's study and said: "I just want to distract you a bit."

And yet, this last chapter of their life story was not simply idyllic. Dorothee's joy in the important things in life and her affirmation of finitude were accompanied by the yearning for the removal of all boundaries and the search for truth and knowledge.

Dorothee Soelle's great final work, *The Silent Cry: Mysticism and Resistance,* summing up all that comprised her life and thought, came about in a laborious struggle, with many cigarillos, a great deal of red wine, and a huge expenditure of her inward and outward self, to the limits of her physical strength. And her attention to the world outside was as passionate as to her inner, the deeper world. In the same way, her attention to the world outside was connected to her search for God in and behind all things. She was still a little bit the Joan of Arc of her adolescence, but now even more like Simone Weil and Dorothy Day—with no coat of armor; thin-skinned, her skin a "window of vulnerability."[5] "When we delve deeply enough into our own situation, we will reach a point where theological reflection becomes necessary. The only way to reach this point when we become aware of our desire for prayer, for hope, for stories of people who have been liberated, is to go deeply enough into our own socio-historical context. . . . We have to reach this point of no return where we will know in a new way that we need God. This is the basis for doing theology."[6]

But this itself is not enough; "knowing in a new way that we need God" is the basis for theopoetics and mysticism. "Mysticism is the experience of the oneness and wholeness of life," wrote Fulbert Steffensky. "Thus mysticism's perception of life, its vision, is also the unrelenting perception of how fragmented life is. Suffering on account of that fragmentation and finding it unbearable is part of mysticism. Finding God fragmented into rich and poor, above and below, sick and healthy, weak and mighty—that is the suffering of the mystics. Resistance . . . grows out of the perception of beauty. And the most enduring and most dangerous resistance is resistance born from beauty"[7]—and from the protest against beauty violated and endangered. Resistance is kindled by that light about which the Gospel of John says that it came into the darkness and yet that the darkness could not overcome it. People in whom the light burns brightly are also gripped by raging anger about the powers of darkness and by the defiant determination never to let darkness rule over the light. Mysticism is resistance—not religious "wellness," but sacred anger and raging, "a raging against the dying of the light," as Beverly Harrison was to say in her memorial address for Dorothee, quoting Dylan Thomas' poem: "Do not go gentle into that good night—rage, rage against the dying of the light."

But that is only one side of it—immersing oneself in God. The other is being held in God's love, the great Wholeness. The light is there even without our raging and struggling. Engraved on Dorothee's tombstone are the words of Psalm 36: "In your light we see the light." It is also written on the family's announcement of Dorothee's death, together with the words: "God and happiness was the last subject she spoke about. She had great dreams, and she embraced the finitude of life."

19

Embracing God

The title of Dorothee's last address, delivered on April 25, 2003, at the *Evangelische Akademie* in Bad Boll, Germany, translates "If You Desire Only Happiness, You Do Not Desire God." To hear the recording of her talk, one would never guess that the speaker was old, not to mention near death. Her voice was clear and firm to the end, as always when she was focused on what inspired her and kept her alive. The next evening she held a reading, offering excerpts from poems and other texts, including the letter to her children: "Don't forget the best! What I mean is that you should praise God sometimes; not always, but yes, sometimes, when you are very happy, so that your happiness flows by itself into gratitude."[1]

But God is not only happiness, and neither is life. "Crossing over a dark river is something we all have to do over and over again," she said in a sermon about Jacob who, on his way home, before crossing the river Jabbok, wrestled with God. "Our life is a journey that is interrupted by painful transitions." God is experienced in them not only as happiness, but also as a hidden and dark power. Everything depends on not allowing this to separate us from God, but to wrestle with God like Jacob and to exclaim at the end, as he did: "I will not let you go unless you bless me. I will not let myself be separated, cut off from the great power of life that carries us."[2]

Whoever desires not only happiness but desires God as well cannot avoid the great laments, questions and pleas that are found in the earliest texts of the Bible: Do not be fragmented, God! Be whole God, and make us whole! Show yourself, God! How long will you remain hidden from us? But then this, too: Yet, I cling to you and say, "You are my God, in whom I hope."

As long as the world is not healed, God is not whole either, but fragmented and hidden and also victimized by violence again and again. The mutuality of the relationship between God and humans eventually leads to the understanding that God needs our help as much as we need God's help to be made whole, to be healed. Yes, death is always at the end of the road, but love is as strong as death. Dorothee affirmed this in an essay written shortly before she died: "It is not you I am afraid of, Mr. Death. . . . What I fear is being left alone if and when my partner, the one with whom I laugh and cry, must leave me. . . . Sometimes I suspect that love—in case we know what we mean when we utter this word—is the only thing you respect. This is why I would like to request that you not separate the two of us."[3] That was Dorothee's great wish at the end, and it was fulfilled. In the evening of April 26, 2003, she and Fulbert were sitting together with good friends in Bad Boll, drinking wine and rejoicing in the evening that they were sharing one with another. Early the next morning, on April 27, Dorothee was rushed to the nearby hospital, having suffered a major heart attack. She died peacefully three hours later. "Steff" was with her to the end, praying Psalms and singing hymns of God and of the crucified brother Jesus:

Ich will hier bei dir stehen, verachte mich doch nicht, von dir will ich nicht gehen, wenn dir dein Herze bricht. Wenn dein Haupt wird erblassen im letzten Todesstoß,	Here I will stand beside Thee, from Thee I will not part; O Savior, do not chide me! When breaks Thy loving heart. When soul and body languish in death's last cold, cruel grasp,

alsdann will ich dich fassen	then, in Thy deepest anguish,
in meinem Arm und Schoß.	Thee in my arms I'll clasp.

Thus sings Paul Gerhardt in his mystical hymn of Passiontide.[4] Dorothee, who loved God and searched for God with all her heart, struggled with and provoked God, found herself united with God in communion with the suffering Christ.

Wenn ich einmal soll scheiden,	Be near me, Lord, when dying,
dann scheide nicht von mir.	O part not Thou from me!
Wenn ich den Tod soll leiden,	And to my succour flying,
so tritt du dann herfür.	come, Lord, then set me free.
Wenn mir am allerbängsten	And when my heart must languish
wird um das Herze sein,	in death's last aweful throe,
dann reiß mich aus den Ängsten	release me from my anguish
kraft deiner Angst und Pein.	by Thine own pain and woe.

These are the last words and sounds to which the dying Dorothee Soelle responded.

Dorothee's lifelong search for God, her unceasing questions about God, brought her not to an answer, but an embrace.

Dorothee Soelle's grave at the Hamburg-Ottensen cemetery: "In your Light we see the Light."

Notes

PREFACE TO THE ENGLISH EDITION

1. Translated from the front jacket of the biography, paraphrasing parts of chapter 1.

PREFACE

1. Translators' note: Soelle initiated the "Political Evensong" (*Politisches Nachtgebet*) in Cologne in 1968, gathering an ecumenical group of Christians to inform one another, meditate, pray, plan, and carry out public actions concerning issues like the Vietnam War, the democratic process in church and society, discrimination against women, and the 1968 invasion of Czechoslovakia. See Dorothee Soelle, *Against the Wind: Memoir of a Radical Christian,* trans. Barbara and Martin Rumscheidt (Minneapolis: Fortress Press, 1999), 37–41.

2. Soelle's husband from 1969 until her death in 2003; former Benedictine monk, later Lutheran theologian; professor of Education and Religious Studies in Hamburg.

3. Professor of New Testament and Feminist Theology, University of Kassel; Adjunct Professor, Pacific Lutheran School of Theology; author and coauthor with Soelle of books on feminist theology.

4. The Christian Peace Conference (CPC), headquartered in Prague with NGO representation at the United Nations in New York, was founded in the early 1960s to articulate the Eastern European churches' concern for peace when the World Council of Churches (Geneva) had not yet recognized its membership.

5. The *Kirchentag* is a biennial mass gathering in a large German city organized by the German Protestant Church for Bible study, worship, lectures, fellowship, and discussion of theological, social, and political issues. It typically attracts youth, church leaders and laypeople, non-church attenders, spiritual seekers, and activists of many faiths and also those of no faith. At the 2011 Dresden *Kirchentag*, the first annual Dorothee Soelle Prize was awarded, followed by an address by the awardee and two workshops led by Renate Wind on the life and work of Soelle.

CHAPTER 1: DREAM ME, GOD

1. Translators' note: Soelle's Bible study on Matthew 25:31-46 at the Dachau Concentration Camp during the 1993 Munich *Kirchentag* bore the title "Träume mich, Gott" [Dream me, God] and concluded with this poem. See Dorothee Soelle, *Träume mich Gott: Geistliche Texte mit lästigen politischen Fragen* (Wuppertal: Hammer, 1995), 21–22. Also in Soelle, *Das Brot der Ermutigung* (Stuttgart: Kreuz, 2008), 206.

2. Translators' note: The banner reading *Ostermarsch* ("Easter March") refers to the annual German anti–nuclear arms protests of the late 1960s modeled after the 1950s British Campaign for Nuclear Disarmament. By the 1980s the marches against stationing of American Pershing II and cruise missiles in Europe fueled the wider peace movement in both Germanies.

3. Translators' note: The 1990 ballad by Klaus Meine, vocalist with the German heavy metal band the Scorpions, celebrates Russian Perestroika and the end of the Cold War, topping worldwide charts in the early 1990s.

4. Translators' note: A high-priority World Council of Churches initiative, the movement for Justice, Peace and Integrity (or Care) of Creation (JPIC) grew out of the 1983 WCC Assembly in Vancouver calling for ecumenical cooperation in these areas. The East German churches were especially active in adopting such a program. Cf. Stephen Brown, *The Transformation of Disaffection into Dissent: The Conciliar Process for Justice, Peace, and the Integrity of Creation in the German Democratic Republic.*

5. Renate Fresow and Vera Sebastian, "Leben, ohne Angst zu haben" [To Live without Being Afraid], texts by Bertolt Brecht, Kurt Tucholsky, et al., music by Hanns Eisler, Concert Program (n.d.)

6. Johannes R. Becher and Jens-Fietje Dwars, *Hundert Gedichte* (Berlin: Aufbau, 2008).

7. Translators' note: The Marxist Socialist Realist aesthetic calls for ideal figures shaped by socialist society.

8. Translators' note: The Moravian Brethren daily lectionary (*Losungen*) is commonly used by Christians in the German-speaking world and in translation worldwide.

CHAPTER 2: COMPAÑERA DOROTHEE SOELLE *PRESENTE!*

1. Bärbel Wartenberg-Potter, Contribution to the Forum Discussion "Vergiss das Beste Nicht!" [Don't Forget the Best!] at the 2003 Memorial Event for Dorothee Soelle, Evangelische Akademie Bad Boll. See note 6 below. See also *Against the Wind: Memoir of a Radical Christian,* trans. Barbara and Martin Rumscheidt (Minneapolis: Fortress Press, 1999), 165–68.

2. Fulbert Steffensky, "Nachwort zu einem Leben," in *Hamburger Universitätsreden, New Series 8,* Zum Gedenken an Dorothee Soelle [In Memory of Dorothee Soelle] (Hamburg: Pressestelle der Universität Hamburg, 2004), 101–8.

3. Steffensky, "Nachwort," 101.

4. Translators' note: Hyphenating verbs like *er-innern* (re-member or re-collect) is unusual, here presumably to emphasize memory becoming an integral part of the inward self.

5. Dorothee Soelle, *The Silent Cry: Mysticism and Resistance,* trans. Barbara and Martin Rumscheidt (Minneapolis: Fortress Press, 2001), 4–5.

6. "The Little Sister of Mysticism," lecture at the Commemorative Event "und ist noch nicht erschienen, was wir sein werden" [and what we shall be has not yet appeared], Dorothee Soelle's Significance for a Future Christianity, April 23–24, 2004, Evangelische Akademie Bad Boll (Text Service Nov 2004): 38.

7. Madres de Plaza de Mayo in Chile and Comadres in El Salvador.

8. The peace movement of this period saw the real possibility of the end of life on earth through wars, environmental destruction, and the exploitation of the Third World.

9. Steffensky, "Nachwort," 102f.

10. Translators' note: Swiss Reformed theologian (1886–1968) and chief author of the 1934 Barmen Declaration, which rejected Nazi control of the German churches.

11. Dietrich Bonhoeffer, *Letters and Papers from Prison,* Dietrich Bonhoeffer Works, vol. 8, ed. John de Gruchy, trans. Barbara and Martin Rumscheidt (Minneapolis: Fortress Press, 2009), 52.

12. Steffensky, "Nachwort," 106.

13. Translators' note: One of the best-known Medieval German mystics (ca. 1260–1326); influential today among postmodern thinkers such as Jacques Derrida and non-Christian mystics like Eckhart Tolle.

CHAPTER 3: IN THE DARKNESS OF A GERMAN ROMANTIC YOUTH

1. Dorothee Soelle, *Against the Wind: Memoir of a Radical Christian,* trans. Barbara and Martin Rumscheidt (Minneapolis: Fortress Press, 1999), 5 (alt trans.), cited as *Memoir.*

2. Ibid., 1.

3. Ibid., 1–2.

4. Ibid., 5.

5. Translators' note: The legal obligation to show absolute loyalty to Adolf Hitler as Leader (*Führer*) at every level of German society.

6. Translators' note: This and the following several paragraphs summarize material from chapters 1–2 of *Against the Wind*. Here, (4) Soelle speaks of growing up with two languages: "At home, there was plain language that named the shootings, torture, and deportations. But for school, where frankness was mortally dangerous, our speech was guarded."

7. Translators' note: "Refusal" (*Verweigerung*), a form of resistance to the Nazi regime that fell short of organized action but comprised "crimes" that could cost one's career or cause arrest, included: not flying the Swastika flag, refusing to give the "Heil Hitler" greeting, or failing to report others' critical remarks or actions against the regime.

8. Translators' note: The German poet Novalis used this key symbol in his romantic novel *Heinrich von Ofterdingen* (1802); it came to represent longing for the Infinite or Universal.

9. Translators' note: Rainer M. Rilke (1875–1926), poet, novelist; born in Prague, traveled to Russia at age twenty-two, worked with sculptor Rodin at the Worpswede artist colony; lived in Paris until World War I.

10. Translators' note: From the epigram "Patmos" by Friedrich Hölderlin (1770–1843).

11. Translators' note: *Das Stundenbuch* (1906) was Rilke's first great poetic work (trans. Anita Barrows and Joanna Macy 1996). Its three "books" address monastic life, pilgrimage, poverty, and death.

12. Translators' note: Goethe's first novel (1774) of a young romantic driven to suicide by unrequited love.

13. Translators' note: Joseph Eichendorff's "Trost der Welt" [Consolation of the World], set to music by Robert Schumann in 1850, was the typical taste of the nineteenth- and early-twentieth-century German Youth Movement, later co-opted by the Nazi Hitler Youth, who sang *Lieder* (romantic art songs) on hiking and camping trips and at *Singabende* (evenings for group singing).

14. *Memoir*, 6. A phrase omitted in the English edition is included here.

15. Translators' note: The path chosen by some writers, artists, and public intellectuals from 1933 to 1945 of retreating into silence or other forms of expression likely to escape the Nazi censors rather than going into exile or endangering their lives.

16. Translators' note: *Memoir*, 7.

17. Ibid., 9 (alt. trans.)

18. Ibid., 7 (alt. trans.)

19. Translators' note: Membership in the *Bund Deutscher Mädel* (League of German Girls)—the girls' division of the Hitler Youth, founded in 1930—was beginning in 1939 compulsory for all ethnically German girls aged ten to eighteen; the pressure to join was intense beginning in 1933, since there was otherwise no access to sports, music, hiking, or other youth activities. Nazi Party membership was mandatory for all public employees, including teachers.

20. *Memoir*, 8. A phrase omitted from this citation is inserted here.

21. Translators' note: Ibid., 6.

22. Ibid., 9–10.

23. Ibid., 10 (alt. trans.)

24. Translators' note: The German term that Soelle chooses here, *Wiedergutmachung* (literally, "making good again"), refers to reparation payments by one party or state to another, in this case by Germany to the victorious powers of World Wars I and II to surviving victims.

25. *Memoir*, 17.

26. Translators' note: *Totensonntag* (literally, "Sunday of the dead"), comparable to the Catholic holy days All Saints and All Souls (November 1 and 2), is observed by German Lutherans the last Sunday of the church year in late November, preceding the first Sunday of Advent.

27. Margaret Zmarlik, "Dorothee Soelle, eine feurige Wolke in der Nacht" [A Cloud of Fire in the Night], Publik-Forum Extra (Oberursel, Feb 26, 2004): 6.

28. Ibid.

CHAPTER 4: SUSPENDED IN NOTHINGNESS

1. Translators' note: From Virginia Woolf, *Orlando: A Biography* (1928).

2. Dorothee Soelle, *Against the Wind: Memoir of a Radical Christian,* trans. Barbara and Martin Rumscheidt (Minneapolis: Fortress Press, 1999), 12 (alt. trans.), cited as *Memoir.*

3. Translators' note: Martin Heidegger (1889–1976), Professor of Philosophy in Freiburg. See *Being and Time,* 1927.

4. Translators' note: Heinrich von Kleist (1777–1811) was a leading north German romantic dramatist and journalist who radically critiqued the injustices of Prussian society.

5. Translators' note: The border region between southwestern Germany and France lost to France after WWII.

6. *Memoir,* 11.

7. Ibid., 12.

8. Ibid., 11. March 1948 diary entry (alt. trans.).

9. Translators' note: "Inner Emigration" refers to writers, artists, intellectuals and others between 1933 and 1945 opposed to the Nazi regime who were able to survive within its territories by remaining silent or by publishing work acceptable to the censors, for example, in historical metaphor.

10. Translators' note: *Memoir,* 19.

11. Ibid., 12.

12. Ibid., 18 (alt. trans.).

13. Ibid., 19. Dorothee's German expression *mein rotzfreches Geschwätz* (literally, "my snotty babble") is typical of her self-deprecating humor in looking back.

14. Translators' note: The German Protestant church *Bekennende Kirche* (BK) that split away from the Nazi "German Christians" in protest against Party control and policies by "confessing" sole allegiance to Jesus Christ.

15. Translators' note: The Councils of Brethren (*Bruderräte*) were the regional governing boards of the Confessing Church; despite the nomenclature they included women.

16. Marie Veit, "Von Bultmann zur Didaktik des Religionsunterrichtes—Eine Testamentsvollstreckung" [From Bultmann to Methods of Religious Education—A Last Will and Testament], Festive Address in Celebration of her Fiftieth Anniversary of Receiving the Doctoral Degree, 18 December 1996, Marburg. Unpublished Ms.: 3.

17. Translators' note: Marburg Professor of Protestant Theology (1884–1976). See chapter 9 of this volume and Soelle, *Political Theology: A Critical Reflection on Rudolf Bultmann* (Philadelphia: Fortress Press, 1971).

18. Veit, Festive Lecture, 1996: 2.

19. Translators' note: *Memoir*, 19.

20. Translators' note: German Pastor and Theologian (1906–1945) arrested in April 1943, imprisoned and executed in the last days of World War II, along with many friends and relatives, for their role in actively planning the overthrow of the Nazi regime. See Bibliography.

21. *Memoir*, 14.

22. Ibid., 14 (alt. trans.).

23. Ibid., 15 (alt. trans.).

24. Ibid., (alt. trans.).

25. Ibid., 16 (alt. trans.).

26. Ibid., 13 (alt. trans.).

27. Ibid., 17.

CHAPTER 5: IN SEARCH OF A NEW HOME

1. Translators' note: Soelle reflects often on the German terms *Heimat, heimatlos, Vaterland, Elternhaus,* and *Zuhause*. All relate to the concept of "home" or "feeling at home." We translate them in context as "home," "homeless" (feeling one has no place to call home, as opposed to lacking shelter), "homeland" for "fatherland," "parental home," and "home."

2. Dorothee Soelle, *Against the Wind: Memoir of a Radical Christian,* trans. Barbara and Martin Rumscheidt (Minneapolis: Fortress Press, 1999), 13, cited as *Memoir.* This sentence is omitted in the longer passage cited from *Memoir*.

3. Translators' note: Allusion to Goethe's classic heroine Iphigenie, whose "soul searches for the land of the Greeks." The immediately preceding passage of *Gegenwind,* omitted in the English edition, includes a 1948 entry from Soelle's diary in which she defends Iphigenie's image of humanity against St. Paul's in Romans (*Gegenwind,* 30).

4. *Memoir*, 13.

5. Ibid.

6. Translators' note: The author's observation about the German preoccupation with rebuilding and "new beginning" holds true in very different ways for capitalist West Germany and socialist East Germany in their formative years. She refers here to the Federal Republic of (West) Germany, which came into existence under military occupation by the Western Powers (Britain, France, the United States) in May 1949 when its constitution was signed in the new capital of Bonn. The Soviet Union occupied what became the German Democratic Republic (East Germany) in 1949 with Berlin as its capital. There, more official attention was paid to the Holocaust and to the war dead, with blame laid generally at the feet of the Western powers. In November 1989 the GDR regime collapsed; in October 1990 the two Germanys signed a Unification Treaty and five states that had comprised the GDR were incorporated into the FRG under its existing constitution.

7. Ibid., 25–26.

8. Translators' note: Much of the Confessing Church's opposition was to Nazi ecclesiastical policies; fewer Confessing Church individuals and churches actively resisted the persecution of Jews and others.

9. Translators' note: Gustav Heinemann (1899–1976) was the third President of the Federal Republic of Germany (1969–1974); he joined the Confessing Church in 1933 and became a major leader in the postwar German Evangelical church, the peace movements and the worldwide ecumenical movement.

10. Translators' note: Martin Niemoeller (1892–1984), at first a national conservative in favor of the Nazis, was later arrested and spent seven years in concentrations camps for his activities as a Confessing Church pastor. After 1945 he became an ardent pacifist, antiwar activist, and ecumenical leader, opening ties to Eastern Europe.

11. Inge Scholl, *The White Rose: Munich 1942–1943*, Introduction by Dorothee Soelle (Middletown: Wesleyan University Press, 1983), x.

12. Translators' note: German *Fremde* ("foreigners, strangers, people not from here"), adjective *fremd* ("alien, strange, foreign, not from here").

13. Translators' note: The first line of the poem quotes the anti-Semitic slogan "Die Juden sind unser Unglück," coined by Heinrich von Treitschke (1880) and popularized in the Nazi propaganda rag *Der Stürmer* beginning in 1923. See Toerne's poem in chapter 15.

14. Volker von Toerne, "Im Lande Vogelfrei," *Gesammelte Gedichte* (Berlin: Wagenbach, 1981), 163.

15. *Memoir*, 20.

16. Ibid.

17. Translators' note: Cf. Gerald Gillespie, ed. and trans., *The Night Watches of Bonaventura*, Edinburgh Bilingual Library 6 (Austin: University of Texas Press, 1971). A work of uncertain authorship, it was traditionally attributed to romantic philosopher Friedrich Schelling. Gillespie credits Soelle's study with successfully raising questions of artistic "intention" and analyzing ironic processes of "unmasking" (Preface, xiii; Introduction, 3).

18. *Memoir*, 20–21.

19. Ibid., 21.

20. Ibid.

21. Ibid.

22. Ibid.

23. Translators' note: Gogarten plays on the German noun '*Art*' ("species, breed"; see Darwin's *Origin of Species*), as well as "breeding" and "manners" (adj. *artig*: well-mannered, well-bred).

24. *Memoir*, 21 (alt. trans.).

25. Margaret Zmarlik, "Die Geschichte einer Freundschaft" [The Story of a Friendship], Publik-Forum Extra (Oberursel, Feb 26, 2004): 8.

26. *Memoir*, 5.

27. Translators' note: Jewish philosopher, essayist, author of *I and Thou* (1923). Born 1878 in Vienna as son of a famous *midrash* scholar. Religious Studies Professor, University of Frankfurt/Main until January, 1933; resigned in protest against Hitler. Left Germany for Palestine 1938, teaching at Hebrew University; died 1965. See chapter 7 for Soelle's encounter with Buber.

CHAPTER 6: AN ESSAY IN THEOLOGY AFTER THE DEATH OF GOD

1. Dorothee Soelle, *Against the Wind: Memoir of a Radical Christian*, trans. Barbara and Martin Rumscheidt (Minneapolis: Fortress Press, 1999), 69, cited as *Memoir*.

2. *Memoir*, 68.

3. From an interview with Mirjam Steffensky in Hamburg, May 16, 2008.

4. *Memoir*, 69.

5. Translators' note: The author correctly observes that *Christ the Representative* is grounded in Soelle's personal life crisis at the time of its writing. At the same time, its theological premise, inseparable from that journey, is the post–World War II theology of the "Death of God" (see Nietzsche's development of this idea in *Thus Spake Zarathustra* (1883–1885) as he asked how post-Christian society could reconstruct its moral values).

6. Translators' note: Allusion to Immanuel Kant's definition of Enlightenment as the human being's departure from self-imposed tutelage (*Unmündigkeit,* "immaturity").

7. Dorothee Soelle, *Christ the Representative: An Essay in Theology after the Death of God* (Philadelphia: Fortress Press, 1968), cited as *Representative.*

8. Translators' note: Bultmann (1884-1976), Professor of Theology at Marburg, aimed with *Kerygma und Mythos* (1948, published in English as *Kerygma and Myth* in 1953), to make the proclamation of the gospel accessible to modern society by stripping it of first-century mythological imagery.

9. *Letters and Papers from Prison,* ed. John de Gruchy (Minneapolis: Fortress Press, 2010), 389–90, cited as *Letters.*

10. *Letters,* 503.

11. Dorothee Soelle, *The Silent Cry: Mysticism and Resistance* (Minneapolis: Fortress Press, 2001), 1–2, cited as *Mysticism.*

12. Translators' note: This line is in verse two of the hymn (EG 316) "Lobe den Herren, den mächtigen König der Ehren" [Praise Ye the Lord, the Almighty, the King of Creation]. Verse two: *Lobe den Herren, der alles so herrlich regieret* [Praise Ye the Lord, who o'er all things so wondrously reigneth].

13. *Representative,* 12.

14. Ibid.

15. *Letters,* 480.

16. See Dietrich Bonhoeffer, "Christians and Heathens," written from Tegel Prison in the summer of 1944, in *Letters,* 460.

17. Dorothee Soelle, *Stellvertretung: Ein Kapitel Theologie nach dem "Tode Gottes,"* 2nd ed. (Stuttgart: Kreuz, 1982), 179. The material Soelle added for the second edition is not included in the English translation of the 1965 edition so is translated here for the first time.

18. Translators' note: The facsimile of Soelle's typescript of the "Credo" reproduced in the German edition of this biography is comprised of seven statements. See *Patience* 22–23 for a translation of the complete poem.

19. *Memoir,* 40.

CHAPTER 7: ENCOUNTERS IN JERUSALEM

1. Dorothee Soelle, *Against the Wind: Memoir of a Radical Christian*, trans. Barbara and Martin Rumscheidt (Minneapolis: Fortress Press, 1999), 18 (alt. trans.), cited as *Memoir*.

2. Dorothee Soelle, "Der Glaube macht alle Bethlehems und Jerusalems besser, als sie sind . . . ," in Michael Brumlik (ed.), Mein Israel, 21 erbetene Interventionen [My Israel. Requested Interviews] (Frankfurt on Main: Fischer Paperback 1998), 55. Cited as *Mein Israel*.

3. *Mein Israel*, 58.

4. Ibid., 55.

5. Dorothee Soelle, Peter Bichsel, Klara Obermüller, Teschuwa, *Umkehr: Zwei Gespräche* [Teshuvah, Conversion. Two Conversations] (Zurich: Pendo, 1989).

6. *Memoir*, 86–87.

7. Interview by the author with Fulbert Steffensky, Hamburg, May 17, 2008.

8. *Memoir*, 87–88.

9. Interview with Fulbert Steffensky, Hamburg, May 17, 2008.

10. *Memoir*, 86.

11. Ibid., 87.

CHAPTER 8: POLITICAL EVENSONG

1. Dorothee Soelle, *Against the Wind: Memoir of a Radical Christian*, trans. Barbara and Martin Rumscheidt (Minneapolis: Fortress Press, 1999), 38, cited as *Memoir*.

2. Translators' note: This Cold War–era conflict involving all of Southeast Asia began in 1955, with U.S. advisors involved from 1950, ground troops increasing from the early 1960s and combat troops from 1965 until their defeat with the fall of Saigon in April 1975. Protests in the United States and worldwide contributed to the pullout.

3. Translators' note: The period of liberalization of media and arts (January–August 1968) under reformist Czech premier Alexander Dubçek, crushed on August 21 when Soviet and Warsaw Pact tanks invaded Prague.

4. Translators' note: From April 1965 to September 1966 United States troops occupied the Dominican Republic.

5. Translators' note: On September 11, 1973, right-wing General Augusto Pinochet of Chile, with U.S. support, led a military coup, ousting the democratically elected government of President Salvador Allende.

6. Maria Mies, "Durch sie wurde ich politisiert," in Margaret Zmarlik, "Dorothee Soelle, eine feurige Wolke in der Nacht" [Dorothee Soelle: A Cloud of Fire in the Night], *Publik-Forum Extra* (Oberursel, Feb 26, 2004): 15.

7. *Memoir,* 39. The referenced section of *Memoir* does not contain the entire article cited here.

8. Dorothee Soelle, *Gegenwind:Erinnerungen* (Hamburg: Hoffmann and Campe, 1995), 81. Translators' note: This passage is not included in the English translation, *Against the Wind: Memoir of a Radical Christian.*

9. From an unpublished manuscript by Fulbert Steffensky, cited with permission.

10. Dorothee Soelle, et al., eds., *Almanach 4 für Literatur und Theologie* (Wuppertal-Barmen: Hammer, 1970), 206–7. See Martin Rumscheidt, "A Calling in a Higher Sense: The Poetics of Dorothee Soelle," in Sarah K. Pinnock, ed., *The Theology of Dorothee Soelle* (Harrisburg: Trinity International, 2003), 71–89.

11. Dietrich Bonhoeffer, *Letters and Papers from Prison,* Dietrich Bonhoeffer Works, vol. 8, ed. John de Gruchy (Minneapolis: Fortress Press, 2009), 389.

12. Translators' note: Peruvian Dominican priest (b. 1928) of Native American and Spanish heritage, author of *A Theology of Liberation* (1971), professing the Gospel of solidarity with the poor.

13. Cf. chapter 6, for the text of "Credo."

14. Statement by Luise Schottroff, August 2, 1974, SWF-TV Broadcast "Blick ins Land."

15. Author Interview with Luise Schottroff, Kassel, April 19, 2008.

16. Translators' note: The German phrase New Testament scholar Käsemann uses ironically here—*über die Dörfer gehen*—is possibly a play on the phrasing in most German translations of the story of the swine herders and shepherds running through city and country (NRSV) to spread the word of Jesus driving the demons out of the swine (Luke 8:34).

17. Dorothee Soelle, *Das Brot der Ermutigung: Gedichte,* Gesammelte Werke, vol. 8 (Stuttgart: Kreuz, 2008), 39. A different English version is in Dorothee Soelle, *Revolutionary Patience,* trans. Rita and Robert Kimber (Maryknoll: Orbis, 1977), 27–28.

CHAPTER 9: *ON N'ARRÊTE PAS LE SOLEIL*—"YOU CAN'T STOP THE SUN"

1. Card from Vietnam, 1972. Kindly provided by Luise Schottroff.

2. Translators' note: This new translation seeks to retain the structure, rhythm, and starkness of Soelle's original. For an earlier version see Dorothee Soelle, *Revolutionary Patience,* trans. Rita and Robert Kimber (Maryknoll: Orbis, 1977), 73, cited as *Patience.*

3. Title and poem slightly altered in this translation. See *Patience,* 77–78.

4. Dorothee Soelle, *Against the Wind: Memoir of a Radical Christian,* trans. Barbara and Martin Rumscheidt (Minneapolis: Fortress Press, 1999), 46, cited as *Memoir.*

5. Translators' note: Allusion to the opening line of the *Internationale*: *Wacht auf, Verdammte dieser Erde* ("Wake up, you wretched of the Earth"). See Frantz Fanon, *The Wretched of the Earth,* 2001, first published in French in 1961.

6. Translators' note: Julia Esquivel (b. 1930), Catholic poet, theologian, and activist, publicly opposed the murders and violence against the indigenous peoples of Guatemala, received death threats and was forced into exile in 1980. Published poetry, lectured and taught worldwide, returned to Guatemala in 1992 to teach and do reconciliation work.

7. Ibid.

8. Julia Esquivel, unpublished 1981 talk at the Ecumenical Center, Bossey, Switzerland.

9. Allusion to Micah 4:3-4, a watchword of peace movements worldwide.

10. *Patience,* 79.

11. Ernesto Cardenal, "Epistle to Monsignor Casaldàliga" in *Zero Hour and Other Documentary Poems,* ed. and trans. Donald D. Walsh (New York: New Directions, 1980), 89 (alt. trans.).

12. Renate Wind, *Bis zur letzten Konsequenz: Die Lebensgeschichte des Camilo Torres* [Taking the Ultimate Risk: The Life of Camilo Torres] (Weinheim: Beltz, 1994), 70f.

13. Ernesto Cardenal, "Listen to My Just Cause Lord" in *Psalms of Struggle and Liberation,* trans. Emily McAnany (New York: Herder, 1971), 29–30 (altered for accuracy and tone based on the Spanish original of the passage cited by Renate Wind in a German adaptation).

14. *Memoir,* 30.

15. Ibid.

16. Dorothee Soelle and Klaus Schmidt, eds., *Christen für den Sozialismus* [Christians for Socialism] (Stuttgart: Kohlhammer, 1975), 12.

17. Soelle, *Die revolutionäre Geduld: Gedichte* (Berlin: Fietkau, 1974), 8. Translators' note: This poem is not included in the English version, *Patience.*

CHAPTER 10: SUFFERING AND PASSION

1. Translators' note: Soelle cites this often-quoted statement by Konstantin Simonov from an interview with the Russian poet in an unnamed documentary on Vietnam, presumably "There is No Foreign Country" (1972). Dorothee Soelle, *Suffering* (Philadelphia: Fortress Press, 1975), 172. Cf. Alfred Andersch and Konstantin Simonov, *Es gibt kein fremdes Leiden: Briefe und Essays zu Krieg und Frieden* [There Is No Alien Suffering: Letters and Essays on War and Peace] (1981). *Fremdes Leiden* literally means "suffering by another."

2. Translators' note: Günter Eich (1907–1972), award-winning lyricist, essayist, translator from Chinese; first published poems written in a U.S. prison camp in 1945 in an effort to resurrect his native language, distorted by lies, for poetry. Cofounder of *Gruppe 47.*

3. Margaret Zmarlik, "Dorothee Soelle, eine feurige Wolke in der Nacht" [Dorothee Soelle: A Cloud of Fire in in the Night], Publik-Forum Extra (Oberursel, Feb 26, 2004): 19.

4. Translators' note: From the final speech of Chilean President Salvador Allende, September 11, 1973, the morning of the fascist military putsch in Santiago de Chile, shortly before his death.

5. Dom Helder Camara, *Essential Writings,* ed. Francis McDonagh (Maryknoll: Orbis, 2009), 120.

6. Dietrich Bonhoeffer, *Letters and Papers from Prison,* Dietrich Bonhoeffer Works, vol. 8, ed. John de Gruchy (Minneapolis: Fortress Press, 2009), 480, cited as *Letters.*

7. Translators' note: Elisabeth Käsemann, b. 1947, a young political scientist and sociologist, daughter of theologian Ernst Käsemann, worked in the slums of Buenos Aires from 1971 until her disappearance, torture and murder by the Argentine military.

8. Dorothee Soelle, *Fliegen lernen: Gedichte* [Learning to Fly: Poems], 6th ed. (Berlin: Fietkau, 1979, 2006), 13.

9. Translators' note: See Dellwo and Baer, eds., *Dass du zwei Tage schweigst unter der Folter* [That You Remain Silent for Two Days When Being Tortured] (Hamburg: Laika, 2010).

10. Bonhoeffer, *Letters*, 478–79.

11. Dorothee Soelle, *Suffering*, trans. Everett R. Kalin (Philadelpia: Fortress Press, 1973), 134–35.

12. Ibid., 138–40.

13. See Ch. 9, n. 6.

14. Translators' note: Buchenwald was a Nazi concentration camp between Erfurt and Weimar, Germany, site of mass extermination of Jews and opponents of the regime; Terezin was a transition camp near Prague used for propaganda purposes to create the impression of good treatment of prisoners despite starvation and eventual deportation to death camps; some inmates were outstanding artists, musicians, and writers whose works survive.

15. Translators' note: Lidice was a Czech village destroyed by the Nazis on June 10, 1942, in reprisal for the killing of SS Leader Reinhard Heydrich.

16. Translators' note: Mutlangen was a U.S. Army airfield near Stuttgart where the first nine of 108 planned NATO Pershing II nuclear missiles were installed in 1983, bringing mass protests to the site.

17. Translators' note: Greenham Common was a former airfield in Berkshire, England, site of a Women's Peace Camp established in the early 1980s where the RAF was stationing nuclear missiles.

18. Dorothee Soelle, *Zivil und Ungehorsam: Gedichte* [Civil and Disobedient: Poems] (Berlin: Fietkau, 1990), 67. Also in Dorothee Soelle, Ursula Baltz-Otto, and Fulbert Steffensky, *Das Brot der Ermutigung: Gedichte*, Gesammelte Werke. [The Bread of Encouragement: Poems, Collected Works], vol. 8 (Freiburg: Kreuz), 114.

CHAPTER 11: JOURNEY

1. Translators' note: The title refers to Soelle's 1975 book *Die Hinreise: Zur religiösen Erfahrung—Texte und Überlegungen* [The Journey: On Religious Experience—Texts and Reflections] published in English as *Death by Bread Alone: Texts and Reflections on Religious Experience*, trans. David L. Scheidt (Philadelphia: Fortress Press, 1978). *Hinreise* implies a destination, while "journey" lacks that precise aspect of travel. The epigraph that we translate here from Wind's citation of *Die Hinreise* is omitted in *Bread*.

2. Dorothee Sölle, *Death by Bread Alone: Texts and Reflections on Religious Experience*, trans. David L. Scheidt (Philadelphia: Fortress Press, 1975), 17–18 (alt. trans.), cited as *Bread*.

3. Ibid., 18.

4. Letter from Dorothee Sölle to Luise Schottroff, March 31, 1975, generously provided to the author by Luise Schottroff.

5. Dorothee Soelle, *Against the Wind: Memoir of a Radical Christian*, trans. Barbara and Martin Rumscheidt (Minneapolis: Fortress Press, 1999), 160 (alt. trans.), cited as *Memoir*.

6. Author's conversation with Luise Schottroff, April 19, 2008, in Kassel.

7. Translators' note: See Bibliography in this volume.

8. *Bread*, 106.

9. Ibid.

10. Cf. Dorothee Soelle, *Und ist noch nicht erschienen, was wir sein werden: Stationen feministischer Theologie* [And What We Shall Be Has Not Yet Been Revealed: Stations of Feminist Theology] (Munich: DTV, 1988).

11. Translators' note: *Bread*, 120–21 and 122–23. Ellipses indicate parts of the text omitted by Renate Wind (alt. trans.), Bible citation is NRSV.

12. Dorothee Soelle, *Ich will nicht auf tausend Messern gehen: Gedichte* [I Don't Want to Walk on a Thousand Knives: Poems] (Munich: DTV, 2d ed. 1987), 145–47, cited as *Knives*.

13. Translators' note: Ellipses indicate sections omitted by Renate Wind.

CHAPTER 12: LEAVING MY MOTHER'S HOME AND MY FATHER'S COUNTRY

1. From the author's interview with Tom F. Driver in New York, October 25, 2007.

2. Ibid.

3. From the author's interview with Janet Walton in New York, October 24, 2007.

4. Beverly Harrison during the panel discussion "In Memory of Dorothee Soelle (1929–2003)" held at the Annual Meeting of the American Academy of Religion (AAR) in Atlanta, 2003.

5. From the author's interview with Janet Walton in New York, March 3, 2003. See Walton's (with Robert McAfee Brown) *Art and Worship: A Vital Connection* (Wilmington: Michael Glazier, 1988), 107–8.

6. Translators' note: Daniel Berrigan (1921–), Jesuit priest, nonviolent peace activist and poet; cofounder with his brother Philip and Trappist monk Thomas Merton of the anti-nuclear Plowshares movement; author of more than twenty books.

7. Dorothee Soelle, *New Yorker Tagebuch* [New York Diary] (Zurich: Pendo, 1987), 28–29.

8. Ibid., 31.

9. Translators' note: Bonhoeffer's 1933 Christology lectures were preserved in the form of student notes in shorthand, later transcribed and reconstructed by scholars and editors and published in German in Dietrich Bonhoeffer Werke, vol. 12, in 1997.

10. For the current English translation see Dietrich Bonhoeffer, "Lectures on Christology," in *Berlin 1932–1933*, Dietrich Bonhoeffer Works, vol. 12, ed. Larry Rasmussen (Minneapolis: Fortress Press, 2009), 299–360.

11. See Craig Nessan and Renate Wind, *Who Is Christ for Us*? (Minneapolis: Fortress Press, 2002).

12. *New Yorker Tagebuch*, 38.

CHAPTER 13: LEARNING TO FLY

1. Dorothee Soelle, "Heart Attack," unpublished poem, April 1981. Translation by Charles Yerkes provided to Renate Wind by Tom Driver of Union Seminary for the English edition of this biography.

2. Dorothee Soelle, *Fliegen lernen: Gedichte.* (Berlin: Fietkau, 1979); *New Yorker Tagebuch* [New York Diary] (Zurich: Pendo, 1987).

3. Translators' note: Soelle's poetry volume *Ich will nicht auf tausend Messern gehen* [I Do Not Want to Walk on a Thousand Knives] was also published that year in a second edition (Munich: Taschenbuch, 1987), including her earlier "Meditationen und Gebrauchstexte" [Meditations and Other Texts], "Revolutionäre Geduld" [Revolutionary Patience], and "Fliegen Lernen" [Learning to Fly].

4. Translators' note: "Frauenzimmer" is an archaic word used only ironically in modern German. In a letter to Helmut Gollwitzer, Karl Barth exclaimed in response to Soelle's book *Christ the Representative:* "Was für ein Frauenzimmer!" [What a woman! What great intelligence and even greater obtuseness!] Karl Barth, *Briefe 1961–1968* (Zurich: TVZ, 1975), 444. The remainder of the author's reported citation could not be verified.

5. Author Interview with Christopher Morse in New York, March 3, 2008.

6. Ibid.

7. Author Interview with Donald Shriver in New York, March 5, 2008.

8. Translators' note: Part of the difficulty of this incident is presumably also a cultural difference; audience participation by such spontaneous responses is common in German public discussion of controversial issues, while this would have presumably seemed rude to many at Union.

9. Dorothee Soelle, "Christofaschismus!" Unpublished Paper (p. 13), provided by Luise Schottroff.

10. Recollections of former students during the panel discussion "In Memory of Dorothee Soelle (1929–2003)" held at the Annual Meeting of the American Academy of Religion (AAR) in Atlanta, 2003.

11. Translators' note: In 1980 the United States ratified the 1951 United Nations Refugee Act, mandating legal entry to the United States for refugees with grounds to fear persecution or death upon return (i.e., by deportation) to their home country. The Sanctuary Movement intended to refute the U.S. government's view that refugees fleeing the wars in Central America were illegal and that protecting them was illegal and to demonstrate openly (1) the biblical injunction to protect the refugee and (2) the legal responsibility of the U.S. government to provide protection for such refugees from war-torn countries such as El Salvador and Guatemala. Sanctuary communities openly granted protection in public defiance of what they considered illegal U.S. government deportation of refugees. The movement's success is still debated but has inspired a rebirth in response to the current situation of undocumented workers.

12. *New Yorker Tagebuch*, 53.

13. Translators' note: Reference to Proverbs 29:18. Cf. Dorothee's book, *Ein Volk ohne Vision geht zugrunde* [A people without a Vision Dies] (Wuppertal: Hammer, 1986), reflecting on this biblical passage.

14. *New Yorker Tagebuch*, 56.

15. Translators' note: Cf. Paul Weinbaum, *Statue of Liberty: The Story Behind the Scenery* (New York: K.C., 2006).

16. *New Yorker Tagebuch*, 90f.

17. *Fliegen lernen*, 17.

18. Swedish American poet, songwriter, and union organizer (1879–1915), executed after being convicted for murder in a disputed case. Memorialized by Paul Robeson, Joan Baez, and others.

19. Jim Wallace, "Remembering Dorothee Soelle," *Religious Socialism*, Fall 2003: 91–92.

CHAPTER 14: BETWEEN WORLDS

1. Translators' note: From a poem by Albert Hayes set to music in 1936 and recorded by artists including Joan Baez, Paul Robeson, and Pete Seeger, among others.

2. Dorothee Soelle, *Gegenwind. Erinnerungen* (Hamburg: Hoffmann and Campe, 1955), 164–66. Translators' note: Only the concluding three sentences were included in the English edition *Against the Wind: Memoir of a Radical Christian*, trans. Barbara and Martin Rumscheidt (Minneapolis: Fortress Press, 1999), 83, cited as *Memoir*.

3. Translators' note: See chapter 8, n. 18.

4. Dorothee Soelle, *New Yorker Tagebuch* [New York Diary] (Zurich: Pendo, 1987), 75.

5. Translators' note: See previous chapter.

6. Ibid., 71.

7. Translators' note: A play on the title of the earliest collection of Soelle's poems, *Revolutionary Patience*, trans. Rita and Robert Kimber (Maryknoll: Orbis, 1977). The publication established Soelle's renown in the art of 'theo-poetics'.

8. Ibid., 19.

9. Fidel Castro, *Fidel and Religion: Conversations with Frei Betto on Marxism and Liberation Theology* (New York: Simon and Schuster, 1987).

10. Dorothee Soelle, "Kuba: Sozialismus und Christentum—Frei Betto in Gesprächen mit Fidel Castro über die Kirche als Schwester der Revolution," *Die Zeit*, 1986, no. 46 (7 November 1986).

11. Translators' note: Rehmann, together with Dorothee Soelle, Jürgen Moltmann, and Fulbert Steffensky, met in 1988 with former representatives of Alexander Dubček in Mariánské Lázně (Czechoslovakia) to restart the Christian-Marxist dialogue.

12. Jan Rehmann, "Christlich-marxistischer Dialog in Perestroika-Zeiten: Zur Wiederaufnahme der Marienbader Gespräche" [Christian-Marxist Dialogue in an Era of Perestroika: Toward Resuming the Marienbad Discussions], *Das Argument*, no. 174, 1989: 237.

13. Jan Rehmann, "Paul Tillich-ein Befreiungstheologe der Ersten Welt? Kritische Anmerkungen zu Dorothee Sölles Tillich-Lektüre" [Paul Tillich—A

First World Liberation Theologian? Critical Reflections on Dorothee Soelle's Reading of Tillich], *Junge Kirche* 1988/2, 19.

14. From the author's conversations with Janet Walton in New York, March 3, 2008, and with Beverly Harrison in Atlanta, November 25, 2003.

15. *New Yorker Tagebuch*, 7–9.

16. *Memoir*, 64.

17. Dorothee Soelle, *Zivil und Ungehorsam: Gedichte* [Civil and Disobedient: Poems] (Berlin: Fietkau, 1990). English version in *Revolutionary Patience*, trans. Rita and Robert Kimber (Maryknoll: Orbis, 1977), 27–28.

CHAPTER 15: THE EARTH BELONGS TO GOD

1. Dorothee Soelle and Luise Schottroff, *Die Erde gehört Gott* (Reinbeck: Rowohlt, 1985), 119, cited as *Erde*.

2. Ibid., 33.

3. Dorothee Soelle, *Against the Wind: Memoir of a Radical Christian*, trans. Barbara and Martin Rumscheidt (Minneapolis: Fortress Press, 1999), 71 (alt. trans.), cited as *Memoir*.

4. Ibid., 67.

5. *Erde*, 8–9.

6. Volker von Törne, *Im Lande Vogelfrei: Gesammelte Gedichte* [Outlaw: Collected Poems] (Berlin: Wagenbach, 1981), 212. Translators' note: *Vogelfrei* is a legal term meaning "outlaw"; as placed in this title it can mean both that the subject feels like an outlaw in the land, and that the land should be "outlawed."

7. Translators' note: Walter Jens (b. 1923 Hamburg), prominent author of bestsellers, literary scholar, literary and Bible translator; Professor of Rhetoric at Tübingen University, president of International German PEN Writers Union, German Academy of the Arts.

8. Translators' note: Peter Härtling (b. 1933 Chemnitz, E. Germany), award-winning West German biographer and author.

9. Translators' note: Heinrich Albertz (1915–1993), born in Breslau, now Poland; anti-Nazi, Protestant pastor, Social Democratic politician and peace activist in West Berlin; mayor of West Berlin 1966–1967.

10. Translators' note: Erhard Eppler (b. 1926 Ulm) Social Democratic politician, writer, public intellectual concerned with international development,

environmental policy and conflict resolution; President of the *Kirchentag* 1980–1981.

11. Dorothee Soelle, *New Yorker Tagebuch* [New York Diary] (Zurich: Pendo, 1987), 66.

12. Translators' note: NRSV translates this verse as: "Where there is no prophecy, the people cast off restraint" and the NEB: "Where there is no vision, the people break loose." Soelle's version is an interpretation of what "casting off restraint" or "breaking loose" implies for the people who do so. Her book *Ein Volk ohne Vision geht zugrunde* (Wuppertal: Hammer, 1986) develops this fully.

13. Ibid., 129–30.

14. Translators' note: Dorothee Soelle, *The Arms Race Kills Even Without War*, trans. Gerhard A. Elston (Philadelphia: Fortress, 1983), and *Memoir*, 146–47.

15. Translators' note: Carl Friedrich von Weizsäcker (1912–2007), originator of the 1957 "Göttingen Declaration" of nuclear physicists opposing the postwar rearmament of Germany; turned down the nomination to run for President of the Federal Republic in deference to his brother Richard; predicted in his last book, *Der bedrohte Frieden* [Peace under Threat] (Munich: Hanser, 1983) that the fall of Communism would lead twenty years later to uncontrolled global capitalism.

16. Translators' note: See Stephen Brown, "The Conciliar Process for JPIC and the New Germany," in *The Ecumenical Review* (Jan–June, 2002), and *The Transformation of Disaffection into Dissent: The Conciliar Process for Justice, Peace and the Integrity of Creation in the German Democratic Republic* (University of Reading dissertation, 2007), published in German in 2009.

17. *Erde*, 39.

18. Translators' note: See Dorothee Soelle, "Untersuchungen zur Struktur der Nachtwachen von Bonaventura" [Studies on the Structure of the Night Watches of Bonaventura] (Göttingen: Vandenhoeck & Ruprecht, 1959). See also ch. 5, n. 6.

19. Translators' note: A different translation of this poem is found in Dorothee Soelle, *On Earth As in Heaven: A Liberation Spirituality of Sharing*, trans. Marc Batko (Louisville: Westminster John Knox, 1993), 99.

CHAPTER 16: THE GOD OF LIBERATION

1. Dorothee Soelle, *Revolutionary Patience,* trans. Rita and Robert Kimber (Maryknoll: Orbis, 1977), 63 (alt trans.).

2. Luise Schottroff, "Come, Read with My Eyes: Dorothee Soelle's Biblical Hermeneutics of Liberation," trans. Barbara and Martin Rumscheidt, in Sarah K. Pinnock, ed., *The Theology of Dorothee Sölle* (Harrisburg: Trinity International, 2003), 47.

3. Dorothee Soelle, "Wege zum Leben in seiner Fülle—Ein zorniges Plädoyer gegen Geld und Gewalt" [Paths to Life in Abundance—An Angry Case against the Rule of Money and Violence], *Die Zeit,* August 19, 1983: 14.

4. *Evangelischer Pressedienst* 213, November 3, 1983.

5. Translators' note: Opus Dei is a controversial conservative Roman Catholic organization founded in 1928 in Spain whose stated aim is to assist people in the practice of spiritual life.

6. Dorothee Soelle, *Against the Wind: Memoir of a Radical Christian,* trans. Barbara and Martin Rumscheidt (Minneapolis: Fortress Press, 1999), 111 (alt. trans.).

CHAPTER 17: MYSTICISM AND RESISTANCE

1. From the author's conversation with Anne Barstow and Tom Driver in New York City, October 24, 2007.

2. Translators' note: The fall of the repressive East German Socialist regime occurred with the opening of the Berlin Wall on November 9, 1989, after years of underground oppositional activity, and then increasingly public protest as Gorbachev's *Glasnost* reforms took hold in Eastern Europe. This great political upheaval and turnaround, called the "Wende" in West German contexts and the "politischer Umbruch" (political shift) by the East German activists who brought it about, culminated in the March, 1990 elections, which were swept by the West German conservative Christian Democratic Union party, and the official Unification Treaty of October 3, 1990. These developments dashed the hopes of the voices for reform within the GDR and for a new democratic constitution rather than a subjection of the GDR to the capitalist economic system.

3. Translators' note: Critical GDR Lutheran theologian Heino Falcke (1921–), a major voice in the church opposition, coined this phrase in an

address entitled "Christus befreit—darum Freiheit für andere" (Christ liberates—Therefore Freedom for Others) at the June 27, 1972, Dresden Synod of the Federation of Protestant Churches in the GDR.

4. Dorothee Soelle, *The Silent Cry: Mysticism and Resistance* (Minneapolis: Fortress Press, 2001), 191, cited as *Mysticism*.

5. Heinz Kahlau, *Ein Flugbrett für Engel: Gedichte* [A Flightboard for Angels: Poems] (Berlin and Weimar: Aufbau, 1977), n.p. [Translators' note: A Flightboard is the wooden surface of a beehive from which the bees take off in flight.]

6. Translators' note: Allusion to the hymn "Jesu meine Freude" [Jesus, Priceless Treasure] *Evangelisches Gesangbuch*, 396, and the line "dennoch bleibst du auch im Leide/Jesu, mein Freude" [and yet, Jesus, you remain my joy even in suffering].

7. *Mysticism*, 148–49 (alt. trans.). Translators' note: Johann Baptiste Metz pointed out in his lecture at the 2000 International Bonhoeffer Conference in Berlin that the concept of *Compassio* also pervades the theology and practice of Dietrich Bonhoeffer.

8. Translators' note: Psalm 73:23; NRSV: "Nevertheless, I am continually with you."

9. *Mysticism*, 195.

10. Dorothee Soelle, *The Mystery of Death*, trans. Barbara and Martin Rumscheidt (Minneapolis: Fortress Press, 2007), 130–31.

CHAPTER 18: DYING FOR LIGHT

1. Dorothee Soelle, *Against the Wind: Memoir of a Radical Christian*, trans. Barbara and Martin Rumscheidt (Minneapolis: Fortress Press, 1999), 161. Translation altered. Cited as *Memoir*.

2. Ibid., 104–5 (alt. trans.).

3. Ibid., iii.

4. Dorothee Soelle and Fulbert Steffensky, *Löse die Fesseln der Ungerechtigkeit: Predigten* [Loose the Bonds of Injustice: Sermons] (Stuttgart: Kreuz, 2004), 218.

5. Translators' note: See Soelle, *Das Fenster der Verwundbarkeit: Theologisch-politische Texte* [The Window of Vulnerability: Theological-Political Texts] (Stuttgart: Kreuz, 1987). On pages 7–8, Soelle refers to the U.S. debate in the late 1970s and early 1980s about closing the perceived gap in the national defense

systems by building intercontinental ballistic (MX) missiles. She chooses this title to argue that windows of vulnerability must remain open to the possibility of relationship, communication, reconciliation, and transcendence.

6. Dorothee Soelle, *On Earth As in Heaven: A Liberation Spirituality of Sharing,* trans. Marc Batko (Louisville: Westminster John Knox, 1993), xi.

7. Dorothee Soelle, *The Silent Cry: Mysticism and Resistance,* trans. Barbara and Martin Rumscheidt (Minneapolis: Fortress Press, 2001), 302 (alt. trans.).

CHAPTER 19: EMBRACING GOD

1. Dorothee Soelle, *Against the Wind: Memoir of a Radical Christian,* trans. Barbara and Martin Rumscheidt (Minneapolis: Fortress Press, 1999), 167 (alt. trans.).

2. Dorothee Soelle and Fulbert Steffensky, *Löse die Fesseln der Ungerechtigkeit: Predigten* [Loose the Bonds of Injustice: Sermons] (Stuttgart: Kreuz, 2004), 244.

3. Dorothee Soelle, *The Mystery of Death,* trans. Barbara and Martin Rumscheidt (Minneapolis: Fortress Press, 2007), 1–2.

4. Translators' note: These are verses 6 and 8 of the hymn "O Haupt, voll Blut und Wunden" (O Sacred Head, now Wounded, 1656) by Paul Gerhardt (1607–1676). See the chorale by the same title in J. S. Bach's *Saint Matthew Passion.*

Works Cited

Works by Dorothee Soelle

Titles that exist only in German are marked with an asterisk after the German title. For a complete list of Soelle's works in English published prior to 2006, see Dianne L. Oliver, ed., *Dorothee Soelle: Essential Writings* (Maryknoll: Orbis, 2006).

Against the Wind: Memoir of a Radical Christian. Translated by Barbara and Martin Rumscheidt. Minneapolis: Fortress Press, 1999. Originally published as *Gegenwind: Erinnerungen* (Munich: Hoffmann und Campe, 1995).

The Arms Race Kills Even without War. Translated by Gerhard A. Elston. Philadelphia: Fortress, 1983. Originally published as *Aufrüstung tötet auch ohne Krieg* (Stuttgart: Kreuz, 1982).

*Das Brot der Ermutigung.** Gesammelte Werke. Vol 8. Edited by Ursula Baltz-Otto and Fulbert Steffensky. Stuttgart: Kreuz, 2008.

Christ the Representative: An Essay in Theology after the Death of God. Translated by David Lewis. Philadelphia: Fortress Press, 1967. Originally published as *Stellvertretung: Ein Kapitel Theologie nach dem "Tode Gottes"* (Stuttgart: Kreuz, 1962, 1982).

*Christen für den Sozialismus** [Christians for Socialism]. Edited with Klaus Schmidt. Stuttgart: Kohlhammer, 1975.

Death by Bread Alone: Texts and Reflections on Religious Experience. Translated by David L. Scheidt. Philadelphia: Fortress Press, 1978. Originally published as *Die Hinreise: Texte und Überlegungen zur religiösen Erfahrung* (Stuttgart: Kreuz, 1975).

*Ein Volk ohne Vision geht zugrunde** [A People without a Vision Will Come to Ruin]. Wuppertal: Hammer, 1986.

*Die Erde gehört Gott: Texte zur Bibelarbeit von Frauen** [The Earth Belongs to God: Texts for Women's Bible Study]. With Luise Schottroff. Reinbeck: Rowohlt, 1985.

"Heart Attack." Unpublished Poem (1981). Translated by Charles Yerkes. Provided to author by Thomas Driver of Union Seminary and printed with permission.

*Ich will nicht auf tausend Messern gehen: Gedichte** [I Don't Want to Walk on a Thousand Knives: Poems]. 2nd edition. Munich: DTV, 1987.

*Loben ohne Lügen: Gedichte** [Praise without Lying: Poems]. Berlin: Fietkau, 2000.

*Löse die Fesseln der Ungerechtigkeit: Predigten** [Loose the Bonds of Injustice: Sermons]. With Fulbert Steffensky. Stuttgart: Kreuz, 2004.

On Earth As in Heaven: A Liberation Spirituality of Sharing. Translated by Marc Batko. Louisville: Westminster John Knox, 1993.

Political Theology: A Critical Reflection on Rudolf Bultmann. Philadelphia: Fortress Press, 1974. Originally published as *Politische Theologie: Auseinandersetzung mit Ruldolf Bultmann* (Stuttgart: Kreuz, 1971).

Revolutionary Patience. Translated by Rita and Robert Kimber. Maryknoll: Orbis, 1977. Originally published as *Meditationen und gebrauchstexte* (Berlin: Fietkau, 1969) and *Die revolutionäre Geduld* (Berlin: Fietkau, 1974).

The Silent Cry: Mysticism and Resistance. Translated by Barbara and Martin Rumscheidt. Minneapolis: Fortress Press, 2001. Originally published as *Mystik und Widerstand: "Du stilles Geschrei"* (Hamburg: Hoffmann and Campe, 1997).

Suffering. Translated by Everett Kalin. Philadelphia: Fortress Press, 1975. Originally published as *Leiden* (Stuttgart: Kreuz, 1973).

*Träume mich Gott: Geistliche Texte mit lästigen politischen Fragen** [Dream Me, God: Spiritual Texts with Burdensome Political Questions]. 2nd Edition. Edited and with an Afterword by Paul Gerhard Schoenborn. Wuppertal: Hammer, 1995.

The Mystery of Death. Translated by Nancy Lukens and Martin Rumscheidt. Minneapolis: Fortress Press, 2007. Originally published as *Mystik des Todes* (Stuttgart: Kreuz: 2005).

The Window of Vulnerability: A Political Spirituality. Translated by Linda M. Maloney. Minneapolis: Fortress Press, 1991. Originally published as *Das Fenster der Verwundbarkeit: Theologisch-politische Texte* (Stuttgart: Kreuz, 1987).

*Und ist noch nicht erschienen, was wir sein werden: Stationen feministischer Theologie** [And What We Shall Be Has Not Yet Been Revealed: Stations of Feminist Theology]. 2nd Edition. Munich: DTV, 1988.

"Untersuchungen zur Struktur der Nachtwachen von Bonaventura"* [Studies on the Structure of the Night Watches of Bonaventura]. Dissertation: Göttingen, 1959.

"Wege zum Leben in seiner Fülle—Ein zorniges Plädoyer gegen Geld und Gewalt"* [Paths to Life in its Fullest: An Outraged Plea against Money and Violence]. *Die Zeit.* August 19, 1983: 14.

*Zivil und Ungehorsam: Gedichte** [Civil and Disobedient: Poems]. Berlin: Fietkau, 1990.

Works by Others

Andersch, Alfred and Konstantin Simonov. *Es gibt kein fremdes Leiden: Briefe und Essays zu Krieg und Frieden** [There Is No Alien Suffering: Letters and Essays on War and Peace]. Schwifting: Galerie, 1981.

Dellwo and Baer, eds. *Dass du zwei Tage schweigst unter der Folter** [That You Remain Silent for Two Days When Being Tortured]. Hamburg: Laika, 2010.

Becher, Johannes R. and Jens-Fietje Dwars. *Hundert Gedichte** [One Hundred Poems]. Berlin: Gebundene Ausgabe, 2008.

Betto, Frei and Fidel Castro. *Fidel and Religion. Castro Talks on Revolution and Religion with Frei* Betto (New York: Simon and Schuster, 1987). Published in German as *Nachtgespräche mit Fidel* [Nocturnal Conversations with Fidel]. Lucerne: Union, 1988.

Bonhoeffer, Dietrich. "After Ten Years." In *Letters and Papers from Prison*. Dietrich Bonhoeffer Works. Vol. 8. Edited by John de Gruchy. Translated by Barbara and Martin Rumscheidt. Minneapolis: Fortress Press, 2010.

Bonhoeffer, Dietrich, "Lectures on Christology." In *Berlin 1932–1933*. Dietrich Bonhoeffer Works, Vol. 12. Edited by Larry Rasmussen. Translated by Isabel Best, David Higgins, and Douglas W. Stott. Minneapolis: Fortress Press, 2009.

Brown, Stephen, "The Conciliar Process for JPIC and the New Germany." In *The Ecumenical Review* (Jan–June, 2002).

Brown, Stephen, "The Transformation of Disaffection into Dissent: The Conciliar Process for Justice, Peace, and the Integrity of Creation in the German Democratic Republic." Dissertation: Reading, United Kingdom, 2007. Expanded version published as *Von der Unzufriedenheit zum Widerspruch* (Frankfurt: Lembeck, 2009).

Brumlik, Micha, ed. *Mein Israel, 21 erbetene Interventionen** [Twenty-One Requested Interventions]. Frankfurt: Fischer, 1998.

Cardenal, Ernesto. "Epistle to Monsignor Casaldàliga." In *Zero Hour and Other Documentary Poems*. Edited and translated by Donald D. Walsh. New York: New Directions, 1980. Originally published as *La hora cero y otros poemas* (Saturno, 1971).

———. *Psalms of Struggle and Liberation*. Translated by Emile G. McAnany. New York: Herder, 1971. Originally published as *Salmos* (Avila: Gran Duque de Alba, 1969).

Fanon, Frantz. *The Wretched of the Earth*. New York: Penguin, 2001.

Fresow, Renate and Vera Sebastian. "Leben, ohne Angst zu haben"* [To Live without Being Afraid"] (n.d.). Concert Program with Texts by Bertolt Brecht, Kurt Tucholsky, and others; music by Hanns Eisler.

Gillespie, Gerald, ed. and trans. *The Night Watches of Bonaventura*. Edinburgh Bilingual Library 6. Austin: University of Texas Press, 1971.

Kahlau, Heinz. *Ein Flugbrett für Engel:* Gedichte.* Berlin: Aufbau, 1977.

McDonagh, Francis, ed. *Dom Helder Camara: Essential Writings*. Modern Spiritual Masters. Maryknoll: Orbis, 2009.

Weinbaum, Paul. *Statue of Liberty: The Story behind the Scenery*. New York: KC, 2006.

Nessan, Craig and Renate Wind. *Wer bist Du, Christus?** Gütersloh: Gütersloher, 2002.

Rehmann, Jan. "Paul Tillich-ein Befreiungstheologe der ersten Welt? Kritische Anmerkungen zu Dorothee Sölles Tillich-Lektüre"* [Paul Tillich—A First World Liberation Theologian? Critical Reflections on Dorothee Sölle's Reading of Tillich]. *Junge Kirche* 1988/2, 19.

Rilke, Rainer Maria. *The Book of Hours: Poems to God.* Translated by Anita Barrows and Joanna Macy. New York: Berkeley, 1996. Originally published as *Das Stundenbuch* (1906).

Scholl, Inge. *The White Rose.* Introduction by Dorothee Soelle. Translated by Arthur R. Schultz. Middletown: Wesleyean University Press, 1983, 2d. edition. Originally published as *Die Weiße Rose* (Frankfurt: Verlag der Frankfurter Hefte, 1952).

Schottroff, Luise. "Come, Read with My Eyes: Dorothee Soelle's Biblical Hermeneutics of Liberation." Translated by Barbara and Martin Rumscheidt. In Sarah Pinnock, ed., *The Theology of Dorothee Soelle*. New York: Continuum, 2003.

*Anstiftung zur Zivilcourage** [Inciting Civil Courage]. Herder: Freiburg, 1983.

Seuse, Heinrich. *Das Büchlein der ewigen Weisheit* [Little Book of Eternal Wisdom]. Translated by Martin Greiner. Leipzig: Insel, 1935.

Steffensky, Fulbert. "Nachwort zu einem Leben." In Hamburger Universitätsreden 8: *Zum Gedenken an Dorothee Soelle*. Hamburg: Pressestelle der Universität Hamburg, 2004.

von Törne, Volker. *Im Lande Vogelfrei: Gesammelte Gedichte** [Outlawed: Collected Poems.] [Exiles in This Land]. Berlin: Wagenbach, 1981.

Wallace, James. "Remembering Dorothee Soelle." In *Religious Socialism*. Fall 2003.

Walton, Janet. *Art and Worship: A Vital Connection*. Collegeville: Michael Glazier, 1988.

von Weizsäcker, Carl Friedrich. *Der bedrohte Frieden** [The Threatened Peace]. Munich: Hanser, 1983.

Wind, Renate. *Bis zur letzten Konsequenz: Die Lebensgeschichte des Camilo Torres** [Taking the Ultimate Risk: The Life of Camilo Torres]. Weinheim: Beltz, 1993.

Zmarzlik, Margot. "Die Geschichte einer Freundschaft"* [The Story of a Friendship]. *Publik-Forum Extra: Dorothee Sölle, eine feurige Wolke in der Nacht* [Dorothee Soelle: A Fiery Cloud in the Night]. Oberursel: Publik-Forum, 2004.

Dorothee Soelle Chronology

1929	Born September 30 in Cologne; fourth of five children of Labor Law Professor and President of Kassel Labor Court Hans Carl Nipperdey and his wife Hildegard
1945	April–May: two-month stay in Jena
1945	Attends Cologne Girls' *Gynnasium,* reading Nietzsche, Gottfried Benn, Martin Heidegger, Albert Camus, Jean-Paul Sartre, and Soeren Kierkegaard
1949	Begins university study of Philosophy, German Literature and Classical Philology in Cologne and Freiburg
1951	Begins university study of Protestant Theology and German Literature in Göttingen with Professor Friedrich Gogarten and others
1954	Passes first doctoral exam (*Staatsexam*). Marries Dietrich Soelle, painter. Takes a position as high-school Religion and German teacher in Cologne
1956	Gives birth to son Martin
1957	Gives birth to daughter Michaela
1960	Freelance work for radio, journals, and periodicals

1961 Gives birth to daughter Caroline

1962 Works as Assistant at Philosophical Institute of Aachen Technological University

1964 Employed for three years as Research Assistant at Cologne University

1965 Separation from husband Dietrich Soelle

1967 Begins lifelong friendship with Heinrich Böll

1968 Begins the Political Evensong in Cologne in response to Vietnam War

1969 Marries Fulbert Steffensky

1970 Gives birth to daughter Mirjam; joins P.E.N. Writers' Organization

1971 Submits successful *Habilitation* (postdoctoral dissertation, qualification for university teaching) to Philosophy Faculty at Cologne University

1972–75 Teaching assignment at Protestant Faculty of University of Mainz

1974 Receives Theodor Heuss Medal for democratic initiative of public importance and social responsibility and engagement

1975–87 Professorship at Union Theological Seminary, New York City

1981 Receives Lessing Prize of the City of Hamburg

1982 Receives Droste-Hülshoff Prize of the City of Meersburg

1985 Sentenced for simple assault at protest against stationing of Pershing II missiles

1987–88 Guest professorship, University of Kassel

1988 Second sentencing for attempted assault at protest against U.S. poison gas arsenals in Germany

1991–92 Guest professorship, University of Basel

1994 Honorary Professorship, University of Hamburg

1994 Engaged in theological, political, and literary writing projects as freelance writer and guest professor, University of Hamburg; travels worldwide on lecture trips

2003 Dies April 27 during a weekend conference in Göppingen; her lecture the evening before her death is titled "On Happiness"